A Dog Life Well Lived

Praise for *A Dog Life Well Lived*

"Entertaining, insightful and heartfelt, *A Dog Life Well Lived* will evoke fond memories of the dogs in your life, whether they are hunting dogs or family dogs. Phillips has had a lifetime of hunting dogs, and he shares his tales of hunting with them from his formative years into his adult life. He's been blessed with some wonderful and memorable dogs, which he brings to life in his delightful new book. If you're a dog lover, *A Dog Life Well Lived* is a must-read."

--Pat Hoglund, Publisher, *Western Hunting Journal*

"For those of us who are confirmed cat fanciers, here's a shocker— you are going to love Rob Phillips' new book, *A Dog Life Well Lived*. Rob is much more than an outdoor columnist. He has blossomed into a seasoned storyteller who writes with warmth and ease, delivering his most poignant prose for his closest companions, his hunting dogs. Phillips will draw you deep into his world of canine bliss. Enjoy the hunt as he pushes you through high grass and brambles, with his trusted Labrador retriever taking the lead, in hot pursuit of yet another pheasant."

--Spencer Hatton, former city editor of the *Yakima Herald-Republic*

A Dog Life Well Lived

Outdoor Adventures with
a Lifetime of Canine Friends

Rob Phillips

Dedication

While I hope everyone who has a chance to read this book finds some enjoyment in it, I really wrote it for my family. I wanted them to know a little more about my early days, and about some of the times—good, as well as trying—I've shared with my dogs for some 60 years.

So, I dedicate this book to them. To my loving and understanding wife Terri. To my son Kyle, who has shared some of the adventures described in this book. And to my son Kevin and his beautiful wife Joi. I am so proud of you all.

Most especially I want to dedicate this book to my one and only grandchild, Ayomi. Hopefully someday she will read this and learn a little more about her old granddad and the great times he had with some really fine dogs.

"I am your friend, your partner, your dog.
You are my life, my love, my leader.
I will be yours, faithful and true, 'til the last beat of my heart."

–Unknown

Chapter 1

"Every boy should have two things: a dog and a mother who lets him have one."

–Robert Benchley

I'd love to tell you that from as far back as I can remember there was always a dog in my life. I'd love to share stories of romping through some distant meadow with my best pal in the world running beside me. I'd love to tell a tale of spending every waking moment with a four-legged friend that followed me everywhere; that waited at the bus stop for me to come home from school; that sat and watched as I played little league baseball; that slept with me, outside or in, and always protected me from whatever evil might be waiting in ambush.

I would love to tell you all these things and more, but I can't. Well, I could, but it would all be one large canine fabrication. Oh, I had a dog as a kid. Or, I should say, my family had a dog for some of my formative years. But from all I can remember, we never were Lassie and Timmy-type buddies.

Truth be told, before our family got a dog, I had no real desire to have one. I wasn't one of those kids who pined for a dog. I never begged my parents for a pet of any kind. None of my friends had a dog, nor did any of my relatives. So, I had never spent much time around dogs. Sure, I watched Lassie and Rin-Tin-Tin on television, and I remember thinking how cool it would be to have a dog pal like those, but actually owning a dog was never that big of a deal to me.

As I think back on it today, part of my lack of desire to have a dog may have been due to the brief but somewhat adverse history I had with them. For the first seven or eight years of my life the only real dog exposure I had was with the neighborhood dogs, some of which had bitten me or wanted to bite me.

For a while when I was in my early school-age years, the neighbor across the street had a great big black Lab-looking dog. It had seemed to me that if it ever got off its chain, it would skip right over the biting and just go ahead and eat me, along with all the other neighborhood kids. I don't remember the name of the big black dog, but I can tell you he had a mean bark and an even meaner growl, with teeth bared and snapping, froth forming at his gums.

As I think back to that ferocious black dog, I have a hard time believing it was actually a Labrador retriever like the neighbors said. I'm not naive enough to think that *all* Labs are friendly dogs, but I've never encountered another one that was so hell-bent on breaking loose from its chain, barking, growling, sneering, and snarling, trying to get to whomever might be walking past.

Even at the tender age of six or seven, I wondered why the neighbors had a dog like that. They never petted it or played with it. The man who owned the house which anchored the dog was a doctor who liked to hunt, but I don't ever remember him taking the dog with him. The big black Cujo just magically appeared one day, attached to the garage by a short length of industrial-sized logging chain. From that moment until the day it just magically disappeared, the dog spread fear near and far. Or at least from my friend Jack Decoto's house to mine.

Let me tell you, when my dad whistled me home for dinner each evening, I gave that hound from Hell a wide, wide berth. Luckily, the black nightmare never was able to pull, dig, chew, or break free from its confines. If it had, I am confident it would have killed me or whoever else may have had the misfortune of being nearby.

Later in life, all grown up and involved in community activities and organizations, I became acquainted with the doctor who lived across the street. He was a big fan of my newspaper columns and would comment on them frequently, sometimes correcting a grammatical error.

Maybe because I repressed the memory of the big black dog chained to his house, I never thought of asking the doctor about the dog. I wish I would have now. Unfortunately, the doctor passed away a number of years ago. He seemed like a nice man. I guess being a doctor just didn't allow him the time needed to spend with any dog, let alone one that had murder on its mind.

Another neighborhood dog not only tried to bite me, it succeeded.

Again, I have no idea what the name of the dog was, but I do remember thinking that it was an ugly little thing. It quickly became less attractive as it motored over to me and immediately clamped down on the back of my leg, right on my Achilles tendon.

Now, in all fairness to the little dachshund, I had invaded his home turf to retrieve an errant baseball, but did it really need to go after my leg? Could it not have just stayed back a few feet and yapped like most other dogs do?

I shook the dog off, ran home to put a couple of bandages on the bite (which had barely broken the skin), and headed back to the ball game.

As I think back on all of it now, my brief history with canines made it an even bigger surprise that my father showed up one summer evening with a little Brittany spaniel puppy. I vividly remember the night my dad brought the wriggling tiny ball of orange and white fur home. He placed the six-week-old puppy on the front lawn, and I thought it was about the neatest thing in the world. She had the softest fur and the sweetest-smelling breath. I was smitten.

Of course, when you get a new dog, the first thing you have to do is come up with a name for it. The puppy was a female, so it had to have a girl's name. This posed a big problem for me because the only girls I knew were part of Mrs. Cushing's second-grade class, and at that point in my life, all girls were yucky. They never wanted to play kickball or baseball or Army, and besides their total lack of interest in everything that I thought was fun, they were *way* smarter than me. They knew how to read and spell and do math, which astounded me to no end and often made me look bad in front of one of my favorite teachers. Frankly, I had very little desire to even get to know any of the girls in my class, and the names I did remember—Kathy and Connie and Mary and Beth—didn't sound like good dog names.

My folks threw different names out, but nothing seemed to fit. Then my mom said, "How about Scamper?" She said it was the name of a Disney cartoon character, and the second I heard the name, I thought it was perfect. So, Scamper it was.

Scamper could have been a good hunting dog. When I was twelve and finally able to get a license and hunt birds with my dad, I remember what a huge desire Scamper had to go. She whined and whimpered and wiggled in excitement to go once she saw the shotguns come out. The only problem was her immense desire matched her body size. In four short years, Scamper had gone from a sleek, hard-running pup to an extremely obese dog.

I do know that those years were very difficult times for my folks and our family. I had a younger sister die due to major birth defects only a few years before Scamper arrived. And then my younger brother was diagnosed with leukemia. In addition to dealing with these challenges, raising three other kids, and keeping a small business running, my dad didn't have much time for hunting. So, Scamper didn't get the attention and exercise she deserved.

Without much exercise and from being overfed, Scamper's weight ballooned. Still, Scamper went bird hunting with us a few times (never very hard or for very long), and most of the good memories I have of her are playing with us kids in the backyard. She romped and played and barked, and then in short order would find a cool spot in the shade of one of the big old apple trees in the backyard and lie down to rest.

The last memories I have of Scamper are of her at the new house we moved to when I was thirteen. She was able to roam the orchards that surrounded our new house and yard, and did so with regularity, but she never went far.

One cold, late December night we returned home from a family holiday gathering to find that someone had broken into our new abode and ransacked the place. They'd stolen all our guns, some TVs and other electronics, along with some jewelry.

Sometime during the break-in the lowlifes must have come face to face with Scamper, who would always bark at strangers. Apparently, she hadn't deterred them much. My guess is they kicked her or ran her out of the house in some manner because when we came home that night she was nowhere to be found.

It wasn't until well after the police had come and gone that the missing Scamper showed up at the back door. She looked none the worse for wear, but we could tell she was *very* happy to see her family in her house instead of some rude, crude robbers. (I remember the thieves even ground out a cigarette in the carpet of my folks' bedroom!)

The whole family was pretty upset for several days after being violated by these criminals, but it only took Scamper a day to fall back into her normal routine of sleeping, eating, and barking at the big, bad world on our behalf.

Not long after that, Scamp went to wherever it is that dogs go when they die. I always felt bad that she'd been born a hunter but never got to do much of what she'd been bred to do. But she had a good life, and she made our life better by being part of it.

Moving to our new house in the country meant starting at a new school in the fall, making new friends, and facing everything that goes with pulling up roots and planting them someplace new. Growing up in a neighborhood with plenty of kids around had always made it easy to find someone to goof around with. But at the new house, where the neighbors were spread out from here to breakfast, finding someone to play a game of catch with, or just to hang out with, was difficult.

My mother said that during our first summer in the new house, I complained a great deal about there being nothing to do. Once, after hearing me complain about it again, my mom suggested I go to the bookmobile and check something out. She might as well have told me to put on a shirt and tie, grab my pocket protector and a hip holster for my calculator, and head down to the mall. What kind of a nerd did she think I was?

Reading, for me, was drudgery. It was work. It was hard and no fun.

I now know this lack of interest in reading was mostly due to a disability where I constantly reversed words on the page and often had to go back and re-read a sentence to make it make sense. Nobody had heard of dyslexia back then, or if they had, that knowledge wasn't available to educators in my small town. If a child had trouble reading, they were just labeled as "slow." And I was slow. Or maybe more accurately, I was a slow reader. It took me forever to read anything and understand it. Because of that, the desire to read was greatly dampened at an early age.

I don't know who made the final decision to go to the bookmobile that day—most likely my mother "made" me go. But I ended up hopping on my bike and heading to the library-on-wheels where it was parked for the afternoon, not far from our house. As I perused the cramped bookshelves, a nice librarian came up and asked me what kind of books I liked to read. I told her that the last book I remembered reading was *Tip & Mittens*, my first-grade primer, but I informed her that I did like to read *Outdoor Life* magazine.

In fact, I loved getting my *Outdoor Life* each month. Even though it was a struggle, I would spend hours looking at the photos and reading the many stories by Jack O'Connor and the other famous writers who told incredible hunting tales. They hunted deer and elk in the West, moose and caribou in the North, game birds all over North America, and then wrote about their adventures. I dreamed about the day when I might be able to do the same. I didn't realize there were books that might similarly pique my interest in the outdoors.

"Have you ever read any books by Jim Kjelgaard?" asked the librarian at the bookmobile.

"Nope," was my response.

The librarian couldn't believe a child about to enter the 8th grade hadn't read any books in seven years of schooling. I told her that if the author she'd mentioned had written something about hunting or fishing, I'd be willing to give it a read.

The book she gave me was *Big Red*, a story about a young man and an Irish setter named Big Red. The boy is put in charge of caring for the dog, and in doing so they end up becoming the best of friends. They experience many adventures, including fighting wolverines and bears, hunting grouse in the Northwoods and more.

I spent hours reading *Big Red*. I then checked out and read Kjelgaard sequels *Irish Red* and *Outlaw Red*. The dogs in those books were amazing to me, and I thought if I were ever to get a hunting dog of my own, it would have to be an Irish setter. Walking behind one of these beautiful dogs as they locked on point to flush a grouse or a quail or a pheasant would be a dream come true.

My parents took immediate notice of my newfound love of reading, and in discussions about the books they discovered my dream of owning an Irish setter as a hunting dog. In fact, our conversations about a new Irish setter hunting dog occurred quite frequently that summer.

Then one day my dad came to me and asked if we could talk.

"About what?" I asked.

"About a new hunting dog," he answered.

This was it. The day I had been dreaming of.

"Sure," I said.

"I know how much you have been wanting an Irish setter," he started. "But we have a chance to get a really nice black Lab pup from Roy Herald."

Roy Herald was a lifelong friend of my dad's, and he had an amazing male black Lab that was a hunting machine. Buck was the dog's name, and he was one of those Labs that hunted just about everything. He would trail and flush and retrieve pheasants like no dog I'd ever seen, and he loved to retrieve ducks from the creeks and drains that we hunted. Put simply, in my limited experience, he was the best hunting dog I had ever been around.

After Dad mentioned the chance of getting one of Buck's pups, I started thinking about hunting with a dog like him. How fun it would be to watch my own dog trail, flush, and retrieve birds. Still, I wasn't quite sure that I wanted a dog that wasn't red, and didn't point, and wasn't the star of my favorite books.

All that changed when my dad showed up the next day with an eleven-week-old black Lab puppy. She was the cutest thing I had ever seen. Cuter, in fact, than Mary McDougal, the blonde girl who had sat in my seventh-grade home room. And when the puppy ran and jumped into my arms, I was sold. There would be no Irish setter in my immediate future.

I don't remember how we came up with the name Tara for the little black bundle of energy, but that is what we named her. And while the pup was supposed to be *my* hunting dog, Tara quickly turned into our family pet.

She lived inside and slept in the little laundry room that was designated as the "mud room"—mostly because when we first moved to the newly constructed home, there was no grass or landscaping anywhere. So, as we entered the house, which featured some fancy, light-colored carpets, we were to take off our muddy shoes and clothes in the mud room. Tara took to sleeping in the little room and would dutifully go there when my dad instructed her to "go to your room." She would lie with her body completely in the room, but her head would stick out into the hall where she could hear and see my brother, sister, and me in the family room.

She also was a hunter, and we took Tara whenever we went—which, as a teenager with a passion for the sport, was not nearly enough if you asked me. In those days, and until I got the freedom of a driver's license when I turned sixteen, I was pretty much at my dad's mercy when it came to how often and where we hunted. Now, don't get me wrong. Dad and I bird hunted some during the fall and winter months, but it seemed those special trips were not nearly as plentiful as I would have liked.

Part of the problem, besides the aforementioned other commitments that my dad had with business and family, was there just weren't many birds around where we lived in the early 1970s. Often, just seeing two or three pheasants seemed like a good day. That dampened my dad's desire some. But being young and never having hunted much before, I didn't care if there were only three birds in the whole state—I wanted to go hunt them.

Throughout my high school years, Tara and I and a few friends would hunt whenever and whatever we could. We'd hunt grouse and doves in September, and pheasants and quail and ducks through the rest of the fall and into winter. We had plenty of good days, some of which included the bagging of a bird or two. But because of low bird populations, and inconsistent marksmanship, the going was much better than the getting.

One year, when I was home on Christmas break from college, a buddy called and asked if I wanted to go chase pheasant. I was always up for a pheasant hunt, so I grabbed the old Model 12 pump shotgun and Tara, and we headed out.

Our timing for the hunt was good. It was mid-week, so not many other hunters were out, and it had snowed about six inches that morning. Perfect conditions for hunting late-season pheasants.

We ended up finding a corn stubble field that was flanked by a brushy draw. The little canyon was full of cattails and some medium-sized willows. Perfect cover for pheasants wanting to get out of the December snow and cold. As we hunted up the draw—me on one side, my friend on the other, Tara working the brush in the middle—I noticed a couple of fresh pheasant tracks. Seeing them got my blood pumping, and I made an extra effort to keep an eye on Tara as she worked in and out of the cover.

Tara was hunting ahead of me and was nowhere near the big, late-season rooster that flushed directly behind me. So, she had very little to do with flushing the sneaky devil. Why he flew at the precise moment he did, I'll never know. I guess he had doubled back on the dog and was thinking he was making an escape out the back door.

Wrong.

Once airborne, the rooster flew straight down the draw in rapid fashion, and by the time I turned and was able to take the shot, he had put thirty yards and a whole pile of willow branches between me and him.

Knowing there wouldn't be a better chance, I sent a load of number six shot through the branches just as the bird was disappearing around another tree.

"You get him?" came a holler from my buddy.

"I don't know," I said. "I don't think so."

I learned early on that you always follow up your shot because you never know, so off I went in the direction the bird flew. I yelled for Tara, but the dog was nowhere to be seen—or heard. I hustled down the draw to where I had last seen the pheasant, but there was nothing there. No feathers, no tracks, and definitely no bird. No Tara either.

"Hmmm," I mumbled to myself. "Guess I missed."

I whistled for Tara and waited for her to come. I listened for the sound of her collar jingling and for the sound of her panting as she ran. Nothing.

"She must still be ahead of us on some other birds," I thought to myself and headed back up the draw.

Just about that time I heard some brush breaking in the bottom of the little canyon below me. I looked down in time to see Tara emerge with a fat rooster pheasant in her mouth.

I was elated. I couldn't believe I had actually hit the pheasant. And even more, I couldn't believe that Tara had somehow made it down that brushy draw ahead of me and had run down the winged rooster. I was happy, but not nearly as happy as Tara. She actually pranced as she carried the big bird to me. Her ears were back, and her tail wagged. She walked around me two or three times before actually letting me grab the bird out of her mouth. No animal is ever happier than a dog born and bred to hunt when it is in the field. That described Tara to a T.

While I was away at college, my dad occasionally took Tara out hunting. He liked to tell the story of an afternoon hunt up in the Wenas (one of his old stomping grounds) where Tara ran down a rooster that had been winged by some other hunter earlier in the day. A photographer from a magazine happened to pull up on a nearby gravel road just in time to see Tara retrieve the bird to Dad. The photographer thought it made for a perfect fall photo and took a bunch of photos of Tara and the bird and my dad in the beautiful autumn colors.

"I didn't tell him I didn't shoot the bird," my dad said as he retold the story. "It's pretty bad when the dog gets more birds than I do."

By the time I'd graduated from college, I was married, living in a different city, and working at a job that took up a good deal of time. That, and the fact that Tara was slowing down some from age and weight (a human-caused problem that resulted from a mom who thought dogs made for good garbage disposals), kept the two of us from hunting much more together. And by the time I did move back near Tara and my folks, the dog was in full retirement.

One of the worst days in my fairly young life was when I got my mom's call one spring afternoon not long after I'd moved back to town.

"Something is wrong with Tara," my mom said shakily. "Your dad is out of town. Can you come get her and take her to the vet?"

A stroke is what our veterinarian said.

"She's not going to get any better," the vet said. "Best if we just put her out of her suffering right now."

Later that night, when my dad returned home, we took the pickaxe and shovel out past the split rail fence and buried Tara next to the yard and orchard where she had spent her whole life.

She was no Big Red, but Tara was a pretty good dog nonetheless. It's amazing how attached you get to a dog. And even though she was supposed to by "my" dog, Tara was really the Phillips family dog, and we all shed a tear when it was her time to go.

Little did I know, I would be faced with similar situations several more times in the years ahead. No matter how many times you have to do it, saying goodbye to a good dog is among the toughest things a person ever has to do.

Chapter 2

"Happiness is a warm puppy."
　　　　　　　　　　　　–Charles Schulz

When I went off to Washington State University (slogan: the best six or seven years of your life), I had to go without Tara. And boy did I miss her. Roommate and longtime buddy Rob Robillard and I hunted miles and miles of ditch lines and brush rows around the wheat fields of the Palouse during our four years at WSU—all without a dog. Actually, we were pretty successful for a couple of dog-less dudes, but there is no telling how many more birds we might have gotten if we had had a dog working with us.

There's also no telling how much better our grades might have been if we had prioritized studying over hunting. But, hey, water under the bridge, right?

When I got out of college and finally was in a place where I could keep one, I got another Lab, and I have basically had one or two dogs ever since.

While some of my dogs have definitely been better hunters than others, all have had their strengths. And I don't even want to think about what my bird hunting might have been like over the past forty-five years without any one of them.

I'll be the first to admit that I am no dog trainer. In fact, after writing about my hunting dog training techniques in one of my weekly columns for the *Yakima Herald-Republic*, discussing what my dogs can and cannot do, I was immediately chastised in the dog-training internet world. You would have thought I was more akin to a dog abuser than a dog lover by the way some of the so-called experts raked me over the coals about what I expected from my dogs and how I let them work.

One internet messenger from some far-off place called me a "rock chucker," which to this day I proudly wear as a badge of pride. The reason for the moniker was my confession to carrying a few rocks in my pocket to help guide my dog, on the rare occasion that they needed it, to a downed bird in a pond or creek. I'm not positive, but it is my guess that I am among the majority, and there are more rock chuckers out there than guys who train their dogs with whistles and hand signals.

My basic dog training philosophy is to make a dog mind and to let them hunt. I don't allow them to get out of range and I hunt them a lot, getting them into birds early and often. Nothing is a better trainer than letting their natural hunting and retrieving instincts take over with help from their human hunting partner to keep them close.

Everyone has their own ideas about how they want it to be when they get married. I'm pretty sure nowhere in her plans of marriage and raising a family did my wife Terri ever envision a slobbering yellow Lab in her happy home. I guess I never really did either.

I did, however, know that at some point when I got out on my own, if I had a place to keep one, I would have a hunting dog. Whether I had a wife and family, well, that was another question entirely. I honestly figured there wasn't a woman out there who would put up with me and all my hunting and fishing. Fortunately, I found a young lady who was fairly amenable to my outdoor pursuits, and she didn't kick up too much of a fuss when I approached her about getting a hunting dog.

Not too much of a fuss is the key phrase here, because she did put up some resistance to having a dog. And looking back on it, I can't blame her.

I was just three years out of WSU, and we had recently moved from a two-bedroom apartment to our first house. More importantly, our first son Kyle was just a year and a half old and toddling around the house and backyard. So, Terri, in her infinite wisdom, felt that a dog, especially a puppy, would be more hindrance than help.

Of course, she was right, and for a while she held off my periodic pleading for a hunting dog. I played up the idea that every young boy should have a dog to grow up with, and that a dog would be a great addition to our family.

Finally, one day when Kyle was two, Terri relented.

I had seen an ad in the paper for purebred, AKC yellow Lab puppies for sale, and when I mentioned it to Terri, she said, "Why don't you go take a look at them?"

That's all I needed. I loaded Kyle in the car, and off we went.

Now, my intention was to not buy the first puppy I saw. In fact, I was pretty set on getting a female Lab. And, after my experience with Tara, I was almost positive I wanted a black Lab.

"We're just going to look at them," I said to Kyle as we drove to the house where the puppies were for sale.

I didn't want to disappoint the child if we ended up not buying a puppy. I also was steeling myself against buying the first dog I saw. But something overcame me when I stood in the living room, looking at the four little male yellow Lab pups. I melted. One of the puppies immediately came up to Kyle, and when he started licking his hands and face, I was sold. Without looking much at the puppies' mama or ever seeing the sire, and without checking any of the pups' health records or their parents' backgrounds, I plopped my hundred-dollar bill down, and out the door we went with the squiggling, wiggling yellow puppy.

Back in 1982, living on one income of maybe $14,000 a year, a hundred dollars was a lot of money. Again, thankfully, Terri didn't say a word about the expenditure. And while she never really bonded with the new four-legged creature in our house, she was, at least, tolerant.

We named the little yellow pup Zebadiah—or Zeb for short. Actually, his AKC registered name was Zeb's Golden Boy. We figured we would just call him Zeb, but most of the time we called him "No Zeb." At other times we called him "Dammit Zeb."

Zeb was a typical puppy. He loved to dig. He loved to chase his tennis ball. And he loved to chew. In fact, it wasn't long before the nice cedar doghouse I had built for him was chewed up from roof to door. We'd give him chew toys and bones to gnaw, but for some reason he worked that doghouse over like he'd been possessed by a beaver.

As young dogs do, Zeb grew rapidly. Even though Kyle was big for his age, the yellow Lab was soon tall enough to stare him straight in the face. Being a puppy, Zeb didn't realize how little it took to bump a toddler to the ground. Every time Zeb would knock Kyle down in his excitement, Terri would give me a look that would freeze Prestone.

"That's why I didn't want to have a dog," she would say very, very tersely.

Honestly, I wouldn't have been surprised if one day when I was away at work, or out of town on business, Zeb not-so-magically disappeared.

Somehow, though, we made it through those early years. By the arrival of our second son Kevin four years later, Zeb was an integral part of our little family. He lived in the backyard and was almost entirely an outside dog. When the boys were out in the back playing in the yard, in their clubhouse, or in the sandbox, Zeb was there. If he pestered the boys too much, and they wanted him out of the way, we would tether Zeb to a tree.

He didn't like being tied up, but it was normally for a very short time, and it didn't take long for him to get used to these short periods of restraint.

Kyle figured out that tying the dog to the tree took care of the problem. Apparently, this train of thought extended to the handling of other things, such as other children who might be bothering him.

Luckily, our good friends, Rob and Julie Robillard, weren't too offended when one afternoon Kyle came in from playing in the sandbox with the Robillards' two-year-old son Jared and asked, "Can we tie up Jared? He's bugging me."

Terri and I laughed nervously as we tried to explain that we never tie up small children in our backyard, and Kyle got the idea after keeping Zeb away during some play times. The Robillards continued to visit, so they must have accepted our apology and explanation.

I started hunting with Zeb when he was just eight or nine months old. And he caught on fairly quickly. He had one little quirk though. Especially when he was younger, he liked to point mice.

The first time Zeb pointed something, I thought it was so cool that I might have a pointing Lab. In those days, pointing Labs were quite a rarity, and the thought of him locking on point on a pheasant or quail was very intriguing to me. But I soon found out that what Zeb pointed was of fur and four tiny legs, not of colorful feathers and a raucous cackle.

In fact, he pointed so many mice in those early years that I soon ignored him when he went on point. I'd just call him off the point, and away he would go in search of a bird or another mouse. And Zeb did find birds. He even pointed birds—something I learned the hard way after having him point so many mice.

I remember the first time he ever pointed a bird. We were pheasant hunting back in my old college stomping grounds, in the wheatfields of the Palouse, when Zeb had just pointed his fifth mouse of the morning. I was starting to get a little perturbed by it all when the yellow dog locked up again.

"Okay," I said to Zeb. "This is enough."

I walked over to the dog, still frozen solid, to give him a good lecturing on the difference between mice and pheasants. Just then, a hen pheasant exploded from in front of his nose. It scared me so badly I just about peed my pants. If the bird had been a rooster, there was no way I would have been able to get a shot off.

Zeb zoomed after the bird and then came back to me with his tongue dragging, panting and happy with what he had done. I praised him, and after that I paid a little more attention to him and his points. He never did lose the frustrating mouse-pointing affliction but did point several more birds over the years.

Most of the time though, Zeb was a flusher. Pheasants are notorious for their running abilities, and in Zeb's second year of hunting, he figured out the trailing game pretty efficiently. He would get hot on the scent of a pheasant and off he would go.

Because I was in my 20s, still young and fit, I could keep up with Zeb most of the time. His nose would hit the ground, his tail would start to whirl, and away he would go with me in hot pursuit. Unless the bird was a marathon runner and had a great head start, I would almost always be within shotgun range when Zeb flushed it. I would be huffing and puffing, but usually I could get a shot or two off as the bird took flight.

While the 1970s were not great years for pheasant hunting in the Yakima Valley, the 1980s offered considerable improvements. Thanks to some good nesting weather several years in a row, and with more nesting cover around, bird populations grew nicely during that time. As it worked out, it was also when Zeb and I hit our prime. We would hunt either with a group of buddies and their dogs or by ourselves just about every weekend of the three-month hunting season.

Zeb grew into a big, muscular, handsome dog. He became a bird-finding machine. During his prime, I bagged an average of thirty wild rooster pheasants a season. Who knows how many quail and ducks we got. Zeb retrieved virtually every one of them.

For the most part, Zeb was a great dog. Besides the normal dog things—like barking at the mailman or peeing on all the flowers and bushes in the backyard, making them sick and stinky—he never gave me any real problems. Oh, except for the time that he almost got me banned from a national motel chain.

My longtime hunting buddy Rob Robillard and I decided it would be fun to go back to the Palouse and hit some of our favorite hunting spots from our college days. Now that we had a dog to work the ditches and draws around the wheat fields, I figured we would bag more birds than ever before.

The Palouse consists of beautiful, rolling hills in the southeast corner of Washington, spilling across the border into Idaho. The landscape is made up of miles and miles of wheat fields littered with overgrown ditches, brushy draws, and little cuts in the hillsides that are too steep to farm, allowing trees, brush, and grass to grow. All of these unfarmed areas are perfect habitat for wild game. In a day's hunt in the region, it is not uncommon to jump whitetail deer, pheasants, Hungarian partridge, coyotes, rabbits, and more.

Back in the 1980s, virtually the entire region was still in an "open to hunting" mode. If it wasn't posted "No Hunting," it was okay to hunt. And a knock on a farmer's door almost always secured permission on the lands that were posted against trespassing.

So, a hunt in the Palouse was planned. We got up at 4 a.m., drove three and a half hours in Rob's little Toyota truck, hunted hard all day, and then headed for a hot meal and a decent place to sleep at one of the motels in nearby Moscow, Idaho.

The plan was for us to stay in the motel while Zeb slept in the back of Rob's truck, under the cover of a canopy. It wasn't cold, and Zeb had worked hard all day, so I figured he would be just fine sleeping in the truck on some remnant carpet pieces. And I think he would have been just fine if it hadn't been for some swampy water he drank or some dead animal he may have eaten during the day's hunt.

Because of our early departure from Yakima and the full day in the field, Rob and I were dead tired when we landed in our motel room. We went to bed early and had only been asleep an hour or so when, somewhere in my subconscious, I heard a horrible howling and yowling. I don't know what the Hound of the Baskervilles sounds like, but this eerie noise might have been it. The sound would have awakened the dead.

Once the fog in my head cleared, I realized it was Zeb howling away.

"What's his problem?" I mumbled to myself as I pulled on some pants and shoes and headed out to the truck. I certainly didn't want him howling all night, waking the rest of the guests of the motel. If he could wake me out of a dead sleep, he most certainly would wake the people in the other rooms.

My initial thought was that Zeb, who was only two years old at the time and unaccustomed to sleeping in the truck, was just lonely for his people. He was definitely happy to see me and enthusiastically jumped out of the truck when I opened the tailgate.

The easiest solution to all of this, or so I thought, was to just let Zeb into the room. So, without giving him the option of heading anywhere else, we walked straight to the room, where I immediately fell back into bed. I just assumed that Zeb would lie down next to me, fall asleep, and we'd be fine. Although the motel had a "no pets" policy, my plan was to sneak Zeb back out to the truck early in the morning. Piece of cake.

My plan was working to perfection until I was just about asleep. From the corner of the room where Zeb was lying, I heard a loud reverberating *f-f-f-f-f-whoosh*, like someone letting the air out of a kid's giant balloon. A second or two later, the first waves of a horrific odor arrived.

"What is that?" Robillard moaned as he came out of dead sleep. "Smells like something died."

"Zeb may have," I said as I groped for the lamp on the nightstand.

When I clicked on the lamp, I saw Zeb sitting with a sheepish look on his face. Beside him was a rather large brown stain on the light gray motel carpet. As I looked at the stain, it started to grow.

"Crap," I hollered, then headed to the door. I didn't know whether to let the dog out or go grab something to try to abate the spreading, stinking mass of diarrhea.

Halfway across the room, I hit the wall. Not a real wall, but a wall of fumes and odors like I have never smelled in my life.

"Oh, my God," I gagged. "Quick, open the window."

I threw open the door, and Zeb flew out just ahead of me. He sprinted to the nearby flower bed and continued evacuating his bowels of the ugliest, smelliest mess I have ever witnessed.

In the meantime, I ran back into the room where Robillard was gagging and coughing. I headed to the bathroom and grabbed the whole rack of towels, then began the futile effort of trying to clean the soiled carpet. At that point, I would have paid a thousand dollars for one of those masks that police medical examiners use when probing people who have been dead for way too long.

On my hands and knees, with white towels on a light-colored carpet, I scrubbed and scrubbed, trying to get the putrid mess out of the flooring. It never happened. Early the next morning, when we loaded all our stuff into the truck and headed out, there were still the shadowy remains of a stain on the carpet, the size of a placemat. And the towels I'd used to clean were still a dingy brown even though I had rinsed and rinsed them in the tub hours before.

"They're going to charge me for a new carpet," I told Robillard as we chugged down the road, headlights off so no one could see us leave. "Probably for a few towels too. I just know it. I don't blame them. They'll most likely ban me from staying with them ever again."

I watched the mail for the next few weeks and months, but a bill for the carpet or carpet cleaning never came. To this day, I wonder what the motel cleaning people thought when they stumbled into the room. The brown stains resembled dried blood, and they might have thought a person was murdered there. For a long time, I honestly believed I would hear from the police, or at the very least, the management of the motel. But I never did.

I also never let Zeb sleep in a motel room again. Over the years I have softened some, and several of my other dogs have snoozed away with me, even up on my bed in various establishments around the West. Luckily, none of them has ever had poor Zeb's stomach issues, caused from drinking or eating whatever it was that he found out on the Palouse.

I wanted to be mad at him, but it was probably as much my fault as it was his. If I had just let him out to do his thing instead of rushing him straight to the motel room, we never would have been in that predicament. I was really glad that I didn't get mad at him, because soon after that he saved my life.

Chapter 3

"If there are no dogs in heaven, then when I die I want to go where they went."

–Will Rogers

The next fall, Zeb and I faced an even more harrowing event in our young lives together. I still today believe it is one of the dumbest things I have ever done. At the time I didn't think it was all that stupid, but a short time after, and in the years that have followed, I realized I made a very poor decision that could have cost me my life.

After getting a degree in Advertising Communications at WSU, I went to work with my father in a successful regional advertising agency. One of our good clients was Yakima Bait Company. The company, famous for making Rooster Tail spinners, FlatFish, Mag Lips, and many other freshwater lures, hired us to do all of their advertising, package design, collateral materials design, and public relations. Part of our job was to place ads in a variety of outdoor and fishing magazines around the country. We also sponsored several regional fishing television programs.

One of the perks of buying thousands and thousands of dollars' worth of ads was occasionally I would be invited to go on an all-expenses-paid hunting or fishing trip, hosted by a magazine or television show.

On this particular occasion, I was invited to go on a hunt not far from home, up in the Columbia Basin area of Eastern Washington. The sales rep's name was Pat Allen, and he had worked out a deal with some waterfowl guides to take us goose hunting one day and duck hunting the second day. Pat also wanted to try some pheasant hunting. Since he knew I had a dog, and that Zeb and I hunted pheasants throughout the season, Pat asked if I would bring Zeb along.

I was happy to oblige. As was Zeb.

We hunted pheasants the first afternoon with some success. Zeb did great as we hunted some cornfields. We shot several roosters, and he had a ball flushing and retrieving the birds.

On the second day, we were to meet the owner of the guide service in Othello, and he would take us to hunt geese.

At the time, my hunting rig was a 1969 Ford Bronco. It was a nice little rig, but even with the 302 V-8 engine, top speed was about seventy miles an hour. The owner of the guide service was driving some fancy German car, and I was to follow him about sixty miles to where we would meet another guide.

We took off from the motel, and before long the taillights of the hunting outfit owner's rig disappeared into the darkness. This was way before cellphones, so I had no idea where I was going when I lost the fancy SUV.

A bit later, I saw the rig parked just off the highway, so I pulled over behind him. He hopped out of his rig, came up to the now-rolled-down window in my Bronco, and chewed on me for a bit.

"You need to keep up," he barked. "We need to get to the field before the geese get there."

"I'm going as fast as this rig will go," I said. "If you have to leave me, leave me. But I can't go any faster."

The guy slowed down, and we made it to the field in plenty of time.

We were going to be hunting that morning from ground blinds. Zeb had hunted ducks with me a few times on the drains around the Yakima Valley, but he had never retrieved geese before, and he'd never been around decoys. Because I hunted mostly upland birds, I hadn't trained Zeb to just sit and watch the birds come into the decoys, waiting for the command to go fetch the downed ducks or geese. So, instead of potentially having him scare off any geese that were coming into the decoy spread, I left him in the rig.

Zeb hated every minute of his confinement, and he let me know by howling as he sat in the back of the Bronco. Luckily, the geese wanted to be right where we were set up, and we had our limits within the first hour of the hunt.

On the third day, we were taken to a large lake to hunt ducks. Our blind was set up high on the canyon wall, above the decoys on the lake below. The ducks would fly in from one end of the lake, and most of the time, they were actually below where we sat in the rock blind.

Over the first hour or so of the hunt, a half-dozen small groups of mallards came into the decoys at our end of the lake, and we shot several birds. Because there was a breeze blowing, and because we were up on the cliffs, the guide would just let the dead birds hit the water, and the breeze would blow them down the lake.

"We'll go pick them up later," the guide said.

Our rigs were parked only a couple hundred yards from the blind, and every time we shot, I would hear Zeb start howling and barking. How could I take him hunting and not let him be part of it for two days in a row? He was having to sit in the truck again, while we were out having fun.

Finally, when there was a break in the action, I asked the guide if I could go grab Zeb and take him down-lake to start retrieving some of the ducks that had floated that way.

The guide must have figured each bird Zeb retrieved would be one fewer for him to find later. He was also probably as tired as I was of hearing Zeb howling. The guide gave me the go-ahead, so I went and released Zeb from his Bronco jail.

What I didn't know was that at the other end of the lake there were also several dozen decoys set out. Because the lake was so deep, the fake birds were anchored in place with large cement blocks.

Being young and naive, I figured I could just send Zeb out into the lake, and he would go get the dead ducks. But it wasn't that simple. Zeb had never been around decoys before, and while I could see several dead ducks floating amongst the decoys, he had no clue which ones I wanted him to retrieve. So, when I sent him out after the first duck I saw floating in the lake, he immediately went out and grabbed a decoy. This normally wouldn't have been a problem, but the decoys were held with thirty feet of cord, tied to a huge weight—a weight too heavy for Zeb to pull.

I can't remember exactly what happened next, but Zeb was bound and determined to bring something back to me, and he couldn't see the dead duck among the decoys. It probably didn't help that I was hollering at him to come, and drop, and fetch. I know he was in the water for a long time.

The other factor in all of this was the temperature. It was cold and getting colder. I don't recall the exact temperature, but I do know the air temperature was well below freezing. And the water must have been in the mid-30s.

Just as I started noticing the biting cold, I saw that Zeb was struggling. His back end was submerged at an unusual angle, and he was all of a sudden fighting to just stay above water. Somehow, he had gotten his back legs tangled in the decoy cord and was in serious trouble.

I looked around for a long stick or something I could use to reach out to him. He was only about twenty yards out, but with nothing around to use, I was pretty much helpless.

Here's when I made a really stupid decision. With no one around to help me if I got into trouble, I stripped to my long johns and went in to try to save him.

I've been in and around water all my life and have always been a strong swimmer. But when I hit that cold water, I felt practically paralyzed. My breath was gone in an instant—a sensation that you must experience to truly understand. I began losing the feeling in my arms and legs. Fast.

The water was well over my head, so there was no wading to be done. I had to swim the twenty yards out to where Zeb was struggling, still holding a decoy in his mouth, flailing away with his front legs.

I'm not sure how—gasping for breath, barely able to move my arms—I got to him. When he saw me in the water near him, he let go of the decoy, and I got his legs free of the rope. From that point on, Zeb pretty much saved me. I grabbed his collar, and he—with not much assistance from me—swam us to shore.

We crawled out of the water. I tore off my wet skivvies, shivering violently, and climbed into my dry clothes. We quickly headed for the Bronco to fire up the heater.

Later that evening, I had a second round of violent shaking, but it was not from the cold. As I relived the whole episode in my mind, I realized how badly the outcome might have been if I had also become tangled in the cords or couldn't make it back to shore. I thought about Terri and our two little boys at home. While it would have been horrible to lose Zeb in that situation, it was definitely not worth risking my life to save him.

I developed a horrible case of walking pneumonia the next day and spent the holidays in bed. Spending time in bed, reliving the ordeal, I realized I'd learned an important lesson. I would never get my dog into a situation where its life might be in danger if it was at all avoidable. Luckily, I have never again been faced with such a decision.

Over his years, Zeb and I hunted ducks dozens of times. He quickly learned, possibly because of that day, the difference between a decoy and a dead duck. In his fairly long life, I don't know how many ducks he retrieved after that day. Hundreds for sure. Through it all, I somehow managed to stay on shore.

Zeb and I had many great hunts together over the years, but a couple come to mind as special.

One was a duck hunt on the Columbia River near Paterson. Three friends and I decided that we would pack four dozen decoys into a walk-in-only portion of the Umatilla National Wildlife Refuge and set up a blind along the river. Our timing was absolutely perfect. The temperature was dropping rapidly as we set up our decoys in a little cove, and by the time we had our tumbleweed blinds set up, the ducks were coming in like crazy.

The wind was blowing so hard, and it was so cold, that the decoys were icing up and tipping over. That didn't matter to the ducks. They still wanted in. We shot and shot that morning. And Zeb retrieved and retrieved. Even with ice forming on his coat, he still would jump into the frigid waters and fetch duck after duck. When it was all said and done, the four of us had twenty-eight ducks and three geese in the bag. Zeb retrieved every one . . . except for one of the geese.

Back in those days, geese were somewhat scarce, so Zeb had never attempted to retrieve one before. Besides the fact that the thing stood as tall as he did and weighed fifteen pounds, the goose had only been winged and was still very much alive when Zeb arrived to pick him up off a frozen back slough.

The goose was hissing and turning circles, and Zeb wasn't quite sure where to grab it. He went for the body of the big bird, and just as he did, the goose bit him on the ear. I heard Zeb let out a loud yelp and watched as he backed away from the bird. He circled and circled the goose, like a mongoose with a cobra. I hollered at him to fetch. He'd turn and look at me, then start circling the goose again.

We played that game for about five minutes. No matter how much I tried to coerce him by yelling "fetch," Zeb wouldn't risk another ear bite. Finally, he gave up and came running back to me. He sat down in the blind and wouldn't budge.

The friend who shot the goose finally risked life and limb to cross the frozen slough and retrieved the bird. The whole while, Zeb sat next to me and watched. It was one of only two times that Zeb didn't retrieve a downed bird.

The other time Zeb wouldn't retrieve a downed bird was on an extremely cold January day when we were jump-shooting ducks along one of the man-made canals in the lower Yakima Valley. The drains, as they are called, stay warm enough even in sub-zero temperatures that they become magnets for waterfowl.

This was back in the 1980s when the Yakima Valley still attracted hundreds of thousands of ducks on their migration south from Canada. All the ponds and lakes in the region were frozen solid, so the ducks liked to land in the warm, flowing drains after feeding in the area's corn stubble fields. If a hunter walked quietly and alertly along the drain, he could sneak up on the ducks as they dabbled along the water's edge, providing some fantastic jump-shooting.

Zeb and I were the only ones dumb enough to be out on the sub-zero morning, I guess, because we had the whole drain to ourselves. We would walk along, the ducks would flush, and I would pick a fat greenhead out of the flock and bust it. Zeb would run down the steep bank, jump into the flowing water, grab the duck, and bring it back. Except, that is, for the last duck of the day.

I had six ducks and needed only one more for a limit. Number seven fell on the high bank on the other side of the drain, and when Zeb got over to it, he picked it up and just stood there looking at me.

"Come on," I encouraged. "Fetch it here."

But he just stood there, ears forward, staring at me.

Finally, he dropped the duck, came down the bank, swam across the drain and back up to me.

"Go get it," I said, and off he went.

We played this little back-and-forth for ten minutes. Zeb going to the duck, picking it up, staring at me, then dropping it before he came back.

"What is wrong with you?" I asked.

But Zeb just looked at me like I was the one who didn't understand.

I finally decided the only way I was going to get the duck was to walk a half mile down the drain, cross over on a foot bridge, and walk back to the bird on the other side. Which is exactly what I did, Zeb following along dutifully. But when we got almost to where the mallard lay, I could see a hawk sitting about where the duck should be. A closer look showed the big hawk perched on the duck. It was picking away at the dark meat of the duck's breast.

It had been unseasonably cold for an extended period, and the hawk was obviously hungry. Much hungrier than I was.

I got within ten yards of that hawk, but it just sat there on the duck. It would look at me. Then it would look at Zeb.

"It's all yours," I finally said to the hawk. "C'mon, Zeb. Let's let him eat in peace."

I have no idea why Zeb decided not to retrieve that one duck. Did he know it was our limit and we would have to go home if he brought the bird back to me? Did he sense that the duck was needed to feed the hawk? I don't know. But it was the last time he didn't retrieve a downed bird to me.

There are so many memorable times with Zeb. He and I grew up together, in a manner of speaking. He was my first real dog. Yes, there had been other dogs in my life, but he and I were together from the time he was eight weeks old. We played together, we hunted together, and, although he spent much of his time in a big backyard in a pleasant neighborhood, we lived together.

Zeb was a healthy dog, although he must have had some arthritis or possibly tendonitis in his front shoulders because at times he would sit on his back legs and rump, then raise his front legs like he was begging for food.

Yes, he was a Lab, and he loved food, but he didn't beg for anything except for a game of fetch with a tennis ball.

Just out of the blue, he would sit up, like it was more comfortable for him sitting that way.

He never seemed in pain, and he ran just fine in the fields, but still, that one little quirk made me wonder what the deal was. I took him to the vet, who said he couldn't find anything that stood out. He figured Zeb must just like to sit that way.

In the many years and many dogs that followed, I learned that they all have their quirks, and even though most were of the same breed, none of them are ever the same.

Ever since I shot my first rooster pheasant when I was thirteen years old, I have kept a diary of my hunts. Actually, it isn't so much a diary as it is just a tally of the birds I have gotten each season.

The first season I hunted pheasants with Zeb, I shot twenty-seven rooster pheasants. There were several years when we got over thirty roosters, and one year, I bagged forty. During the twelve years we hunted together, I shot nearly three hundred pheasants with Zeb searching, trailing, flushing and retrieving virtually every one.

We were a team. Off he'd go on a scent, and I'd be hot on his tail. There were times when I just couldn't keep up, but most of the time I was able to stay with him until he flushed the bird. For me, and I know for him, it was the good old days.

Zeb started slowing down when he was ten, and even though it was tougher for him to get through the thick brush and he'd lost the speed of his youth, he still loved trying to pin down an old wily rooster.

The spring of his twelfth year he really slowed. He started losing weight and slept almost all the time. One bright sunny morning as I watched him in the backyard, Zeb stood up and then fell down. When I went out to see what was wrong, he just lay there. His tail still wagged as I petted him and talked to him, but even with all the encouragement I could muster, he couldn't get back up.

It was time. I knew it, and he knew it.

We made the drive to the vet clinic, Zeb's head in my lap. I carried him in, spent a few minutes loving on him as the vet did his thing, and then he went peacefully to eternal sleep. Later that afternoon, after my son Kyle got out of school, we drove Zeb out to one of our favorite hunting spots and buried him under a tree.

To this day when I drive by that spot, I think about that yellow dog and the great times we had together. He may not have been my best hunting dog, but Zeb was pretty darned good. He was my first and I'll never forget him and the joy he brought into our lives.

Chapter 4

"If you don't have a dog—at least one—there is not necessarily anything wrong with you, but there may be something wrong with your life."

–Vincent van Gogh

I had never given much thought to owning more than one dog at a time. Our yellow Lab, Zeb, was basically everything I needed in a hunting dog and companion.

Then one day, I received an out-of-the-blue call from my good friend Virg Umbarger.

"I want you to think about something," Virg said when we finally got down to the nuts and bolts of the reason for the call. "If you will have her, I want you to have Sam."

Samantha, or Sam for short, was his four-year-old black Lab. I had hunted with Virg and Sam a time or two and was extremely impressed with how hard she worked. So, I couldn't believe it when he said he wanted me to have his hunting dog.

"Why?" was my obvious response.

"We're moving to a smaller house in the city without much room for a dog," Virg explained. "And I want her to be with someone who will hunt her."

"Let me check with Terri," I said.

Two days later, Sam was in our backyard, lounging with the aging Zeb in the shade of our giant willow tree, acting like this was her forever home.

"I can't believe how she has taken to being here with us," Terri said to me a week or so after Sam moved in. "It's like she knows this is where she belongs."

Actually, we were Sam's third adoptive home. She had been raised and trained by a local dentist who had other dogs. Sam hadn't fit into the pack for some reason. So, knowing Virg hunted, he gave Sam to him.

The change in scenery didn't seem to bother Sam much. She loved our place, and because she loved to hunt, we fit together just perfectly.

Besides being a hard hunter, Sam was one of the sweetest dogs you would ever meet. I never had to scold her because she never did anything that needed scolding. She was incredibly intelligent and just seemed to know what I wanted.

Like most Labs, Sam was a retrieving machine. She absolutely loved to retrieve. She'd retrieve any kind of bird, ball, stick, rock, or anything else you wanted her to fetch. And, as I quickly found out one day by accident, she could climb trees.

I was in the backyard, throwing a ball for her. During one toss, the ball slipped, and I inadvertently threw it into the crook of our big willow tree. The ball disappeared into the hollow there, and a second later, Sam was scrambling up the trunk like some giant black squirrel. She reached the big rounded-out area where the ball had lodged in the tree, grabbed it, and scurried back down the trunk to have me throw it again.

From then on, during our daily fetching fun, I would throw a ball or two up the tree just to watch Sam climb it, which she did each time with the ease of a cat.

It was because of this same determination that Sam rarely lost a wounded bird. And hardly ever did a running bird escape her. If she had to run a mile to flush some smart old rooster, she would do it with pleasure. Then she'd come back for another, all without so much as stopping for a pat on the side or a rubbing of her ear. When it came to hunting, Sam was all business.

But sit down next to her in the backyard, or let her in the house for some quality family time, and she was relentless in her nuzzling and nudging to get someone, anyone, to pet her.

It was this never-give-up, hell-bent-on-finding-the-bird attitude that got Sam into trouble one fine fall day not long after she came into my life.

My dad and I were hunting pheasants in an old hop yard. The Yakima Valley is the top hop-growing region in the world, but at this time, in the early nineties, many hop farmers had let their hop yards go fallow. Some were even tearing out the fields, which look like giant vineyards with poles that stand fourteen feet high, spread evenly throughout the fields.

On this particular day, we were hunting along a small ditch that ran through one of these old hop yards. The field and the edge of the ditch were overgrown with weeds, making perfect cover for pheasants. When I had hunted it earlier in the season, it produced several birds.

Hunting any overgrown field, there is always a chance of running into discarded garbage, broken glass, old farm equipment, and fencing that can injure a dog if they aren't careful.

But when Sam took off on the hot scent of a pheasant, then disappeared into some longer weeds and started yelping non-stop, I couldn't figure out what in the world she had gotten herself into.

The only thing I could think of was that she had gotten her foot caught in a coyote trap. I was hunting with a friend once who had a dog get a foot caught in a trap, and she yowled and yelped just like Sam was doing until we got there and released her from the trap.

If only it had been that easy. When I got to Sam, I couldn't believe my eyes. Somehow, she had hit one of the heavy metal hop pole guy wires that had been cut off a couple feet above the ground. She had run the heavy wire, more the size of rebar than actual wire, into her chest and out her side. She was literally impaled on the wire. And, as one could imagine, she did not like it. Besides the pain, she was stuck, and the harder she struggled the madder she got.

My first reaction was that I was going to have to put her out of her misery right then and there. The thought of shooting such a beautiful, great hunting dog made me sick to my stomach. I couldn't figure out how anything could live after being skewered like she was.

But as I got closer and calmed her some, I could see no bleeding, no internal organs hanging out. Even though the sight was still gruesome, it wasn't nearly as bad as I first thought.

About that time, my dad arrived. When he saw Sam stuck on the wire, I thought he was going to pass out.

"Here's what we need to do," I said to him. "You hold Sam while I try to pull the wire out."

Easier said than done.

First, the guy wire was firmly set in the ground and was not moving. Second, Sam was not being terribly helpful.

Plan B.

"You hang onto the wire," I said to Dad. "And I'll try to slide her off."

Again, easier said than done, but eventually that is what we did.

I figured as soon as I set her free of the wire, blood would start shooting everywhere, and we'd have an even bigger problem on our hands.

But that didn't happen. In fact, Sam, glad to be free of whatever evil thing it was that had her in its grasp, seemed no worse for wear.

"Can you run and get the rig while I stay here and keep her calm?" I asked Dad.

I figured Sam would need to be rushed to the veterinarian immediately if I was going to save her. I thought about carrying her out, but it was going to be quicker and easier to bring the rig to her.

While Dad went to bring the truck around, I watched Sam. She seemed to be walking just fine. In fact, once she smelled the pheasant again, she was ready to take off and get the bird that had put her in this predicament in the first place.

"No, you don't," I said to her, and we sat and waited for Dad and the truck.

By the time we got Sam to the vet, she seemed just fine. I couldn't understand how a dog that had had a half-inch round wire run into her chest and out her side could be that fine until the doctor took a look at her and explained what he thought had happened.

"Looks like the wire glanced off her breastbone and ran along her ribs," he said. "I'll clean the wounds and give her a few stitches, and she should be just fine."

I couldn't believe it. And to think, I'd actually considered shooting her as she struggled on the wire.

Within a couple weeks, Sam was as good as new and hunting as hard as ever.

The only time I ever saw Sam slow down was during a hunt in South Dakota.

A group of friends from our local Pheasants Forever chapter had put together a trip to the Mecca of all pheasant hunting.

Through one of our local members, who had grown up in South Dakota and had family and friends there, we were able to find plenty of places to hunt. And even though it was an off year for pheasants in the Dakotas—bird numbers were down some seventy percent—it was still fantastic hunting for a bunch of bird-hunting fanatics from Washington State.

We hunted hard, and Sam and the other dogs did just great. They were in heaven too, with lots of birds to find, flush, and retrieve.

The only time Sam didn't retrieve one of my birds on that trip was when I shot a rooster on a farm near the city of Winner. The farm was typical for South Dakota with a few cows and pigs milling about in the corrals around the barns, and the surrounding rolling hills covered in corn, sunflowers, and CRP fields.

Because there are very few mountains, or any other discernable topography in South Dakota, the wind blows pretty much 24-7. In an effort to keep their fields, livestock, and homes from blowing away, most South Dakota farmers plant what are known as "wind breaks." These breaks are basically rows and rows of trees—usually coniferous, but not always—planted closely together in long lines on the upwind side of the house and barns. In addition to blocking the wind, these rows of trees are great places for pheasants to weather the storms and find protection from birds of prey and other predators.

The wind break on the farm we were hunting sat just to the west of the barns and corrals. And because it was such good cover, we decided that some of us should run the dogs up through there while a couple of us stood on the perimeter to try and shoot at the birds that flew out the sides or end.

Our plan worked to perfection. I was a blocker, with Sam sitting patiently at my side. In a matter of minutes, I had dropped two fat roosters. Sam happily retrieved each to me and sat to wait for the next one. It was like she had done this her whole life.

I only needed one more pheasant for my limit. The next bird to come out of the wind break was another rooster, and it flew out of the corner of the trees over the barns and corrals. When the bird safely cleared the buildings, I took my shot, and it folded neatly on the other side. Sam hurried around to retrieve the bird with me following, not knowing exactly where the bird fell. We quickly discovered the rooster had fallen smack dab in the middle of a large, fenced corral that was inhabited by a dozen or so pigs. So, I guess technically it was a pigsty.

Now, I'm not so much a city boy that I haven't been around livestock. But up until then, I had never been around hogs. I knew they can be ferocious when protecting their young, and the last thing I wanted was for Sam to jump in there and get attacked by a bunch of hogs. I also knew that hogs would eat just about anything, including chickens and other fowl. So, as soon as I saw my bird in the middle of the pen, I figured I had better get in there and get it out before it became hog hash.

As I climbed up over the sturdy fence to go into the pen, I wondered just how ornery this group of hogs might be. They didn't look overly mean. In fact, if anything, they looked a bit perplexed. I'm sure the thunder of gunfire, and then having a nice plump rooster pheasant fall from the heavens into their place of residence, was more than their pig brains could comprehend.

They seemed to be cyphering out the situation rapidly, so while they all stood shoulder to shoulder in a line, staring at the bird, I jumped the fence and started to run toward it. My dash came to a standstill before it started though, because when I landed in the muck of the pig pen, I sunk clear over my boot tops.

It was somewhere about this time that the stench hit me. I have a pretty strong stomach, but the odor was overpowering. It was horrific. As I struggled to move my feet, I started to dry heave.

Sam sat just outside the pen, peering through the slats, wondering what in the world was happening.

Now the hogs were really in a quandary. Not thirty seconds after a dead pheasant plops down amongst them, here comes some strange dude all decked out in orange, making weird puking sounds.

I guess it was just enough to keep them at bay, so I slogged over to the pheasant, picked it out of the muck, and quickly made my escape. The bird was half-covered in pig slop, and when I grabbed it, the horrible smell immediately permeated the skin of my hand.

The stench, as I would find out later, also adhered permanently to the leather of my boots and to the fabric of my britches. Both went into the trash immediately upon arriving home.

"Those things are NOT coming into my house," I remember my wife Terri saying when I returned home from the trip.

I think if we'd lived in the country and had a burn barrel, those fine hunting clothes and shoes would have been burned posthaste.

After I made my slow-motion, pig slop-hindered escape from the pig pen, the guys decided to grab some lunch at the local café. Of course, my friends were razzing me about the strong odor wafting off my clothing, but I never figured a bunch of farmers in South Dakota, dining at the local eatery, would be so offended by the stench.

The second the waitress showed up at our table, she blurted out, "Good Lord, what is that awful smell?"

"Oh, that's just Rob," one of the guys said, who then went about reading the menu like he heard that question all the time.

I remember they let me stay and eat my meal. But there was an obvious ring of empty tables around ours.

Later, as we paid our check, the lady who took our money (with her face all scrunched up, nose in the air) told us thanks. As the other guys were walking out the door, she snuck behind me and whispered, "Our dining guests would appreciate if you would not come back."

It was on the third day of our hunt in South Dakota that we happened into a side hill that was, unbeknownst to us, full of sand burrs.

Now, we have cockleburs and puncturevine burrs in our part of the world, but never before had I seen something so gruesome as these sand burrs. The spikes on these evil little seeds were at least an inch long. And they were everywhere.

As soon as Sam and the other dogs hit the sand burrs, they froze. Sam had them in every paw, and I literally had to pick her up and carry her out of the area, and then lay her down to pull the burrs out of her feet.

She went on hunting without any problems that day, but the next morning when I let her out of her crate, Sam was visibly in pain. She walked like she was stepping on broken glass. It hurt her to put each foot down on every step she took.

"No need for you to hunt today," I said to Sam as I let her back in the comfy straw of her crate.

There was no argument from her. Normally, if I ever left her in the truck on a hunting trip, she would whine and howl like she was being left for good. But on that day, the only day Sam ever took off, she seemed quite content to lie in the warm rig and rest her sore feet.

Sam hunted hard for me for another four years. And I was extremely grateful to have her because she arrived in my life about the time my yellow Lab Zeb was slowing down. In fact, I retired

Zeb a short time after Sam arrived and would have loved to hunt with her longer. Her life and her hunting were cut short though.

One summer day when Sam was just eight years old, I looked out in the back and saw her limping. Zeb was gone at that point, and I had added yet another hunting dog to my pack, a German longhaired pointer named Meika. Sam and Meika were always playing, and I just figured that Sam had pulled a muscle or tweaked a joint in one of their romps around the backyard.

I kept an eye on Sam, and when the limping got worse, I took her to the vet to see what the problem might be.

"She has bone cancer," the vet said after running a whole slew of tests and multiple x-rays.

I couldn't believe my ears. I asked what we could do to get her through this. His response was grim. He told me that there were several things we could try, but in all likelihood, none of it would save her life. The best thing we could do was put her out of her pain and misery.

They say that every man has one great hunting dog in his life. Sam may have been it for me. My first Lab Zeb was a competent hunter and a great companion for many years. And several of the dogs that have come into my life since have been very good hunters. But I still think Sam may have been the best.

Like I had done with Zeb only a few years before, I took Sam down to one of the fields that she loved to hunt so much and buried her there. I was so privileged to share part of her life. We adopted her, and without even a second thought, Sam adopted us. There are plenty of good memories of her, time spent in the field and with her nuzzling for some petting. She was smart as a whip and had a burning desire that only cancer could extinguish. Our time together was way too short, but I was happy to have had the time we did.

Chapter 5

"The bond with a true dog is as lasting as the ties of this earth will ever be."

–Konrad Lorenz

After Zeb's death, it was pretty much just Sam and me when it came to hunting. I still wasn't of the mindset of having two dogs. That all changed when an acquaintance in our local Pheasants Forever group showed up at my house unannounced one evening. In his arms was a beautiful little white and brown puppy with the sweetest smelling breath and the softest fur.

"What's up?" I asked as the friend handed me the puppy.

"I think you need a German longhaired pointer," he said.

Now, other than the Brittany spaniel our family had when I was a kid, I had never hunted with, nor had I spent much time around, any dogs other than Labrador retrievers. I'd had an obsession with owning an Irish setter at one point in my young life, but once I started hunting around and living with Labs, I figured there was no other dog for me.

"I don't know," I said to the friend. "I know nothing about hunting with or training pointers."

Of course, the guy gave me the total sales pitch. He said that with as much hunting as I did, Mother Nature—along with the dog's bred-in instinct and traits—would pretty much take over.

"You'll be great together," he said.

And, when it was all said and done, he was right.

To add to the intrigue of this puppy, he went back to his truck and brought an old fishing rod out, a pheasant wing tethered to it. I set the puppy down, and the guy dangled the wing in front of her. The little brown and white pup locked up on point on the wing. Boom, I was sold.

I don't think Terri was quite as enamored with the puppy, but my sons Kyle and Kevin were. The boys thought she was just about the greatest thing ever.

As I think back on it now, up to that point the only other dog we had gotten as a pup was our first yellow Lab, Zeb. Kevin hadn't been born then, and Kyle was too young to remember much of Zeb's early years. So having a puppy was a novelty for them. They loved playing with the new little bundle of energy.

Naming the pup was the first chore. The breeder, for obvious reasons, had chosen German names like Gretchen and Hans as names for his dogs. I didn't know many German names, but I once had met a Rotary exchange student from Germany whose name was Meika, so I threw that out as an option. Everyone loved it, and Meika (pronounced "Mike-ah") it was.

From day one, Meika was hell on wheels. I wouldn't say that she was hyper like some of the hard-running pointer breeds I have seen, but she was definitely active. If it moved, she would hunt it. And there was never any doubt that she was going to be a hunter. She was pointing a pheasant wing on the end of a fishing rod before she could jump up on the front porch. And a harder-working, more focused hunter you would never find.

Meika became a member of the Phillips family in the spring of 1992, and after working with her throughout the summer, she was more than ready to hunt come October. In fact, even though she was barely ten months old, she seemed to know innately how to find birds. Meika pointed her first of many pheasants and quail on opening day.

It was the same year that my oldest son Kyle started to hunt. He was just twelve then, and he and Meika were going to experience their first opening day of bird season together. My dad and Kyle and I started the day hunting in an old, neglected apple orchard. We hadn't gone fifty yards into the long grass when Meika went on point. Kyle walked up to the dog, and a young rooster pheasant erupted out of the grass a couple feet in front of them. To everyone's amazement, the bird went down when Kyle shot, and Meika ran to retrieve the bird.

I was not quite as amazed about Meika pointing or retrieving the bird as I was about Kyle hitting it. It had taken me two years of misses before I shot my first rooster.

As good a nose as she had, and as hard a hunter as she was, Meika still had some faults.

For one thing, she could be a bit ornery. If a group of us were all sitting around after a hunt, Meika would get very protective of me and the birds we might have in the bag. She would sit as close to me as possible and growl at any dog that came close to us. She would even snarl and nip if the dog got too close.

She was definitely a one-man dog. She always wanted to be next to me, no matter where we were or what we were doing. When we were hunting a field, she would always keep me in sight. She would hunt along and occasionally turn and jump in the air to look for me. I could always keep track of her too, as I watched her jump up, brown ears flopping as she looked for me. Then, as soon as she saw me, she would resume her hunting duties.

If she ever did lose me, which happened now and again, she would sit down at the edge of the field and howl like you've never heard a dog howl before. And she wouldn't quit howling until I came to the rescue. None of the other hunters in our party would suffice either. It had to be me. And when I came to her rescue, she was the happiest little dog around.

I was her man, and she was my dog.

Yes, occasionally Meika would hunt with Kyle if I wasn't around. And once, in her later years, she went with Doug Jewett and his son Brandon to help them find birds during a youth hunt. Doug said she searched for me for the first hour or so, but when it was apparent I wasn't going to be coming around anytime soon, Meika went out and found pheasant after pheasant for Brandon.

As much as she enjoyed hunting pheasants, there were other things Meika liked to hunt. She hunted quail, chukar, and even ducks. During the few waterfowl hunts we made over the years, Meika would heartily swim into a lake or river to make retrieve after retrieve.

On one particular hunt, down on the big waters of the Columbia River, I was amazed at how quickly she took to swimming way out in the fast-flowing river. She picked up lots of downed ducks, many times even beating my buddy's Labrador to the fowl.

Even with all the bird hunting we did during her long life, cats may have been Meika's favorite pursuit. Bred in Germany to hunt pretty much anything wild, longhaired pointers have been described as "versatile" hunters, meaning they can hunt most game birds *and* animals, including deer, foxes, and even wild cats. Being just a second-generation dog from the old country, all those traits were pulsing through Meika's veins. Once in a while, they overcame her.

One time when we were hunting pheasants and Hungarian partridge in the Palouse, I saw a flash of movement way ahead of us. Thinking it might be a wily old rooster, I took a closer look. The flash of movement had actually come from a feral cat that was crossing some railroad tracks we were hunting. About that time, Meika hit the scent path of a pheasant and took off down the track siding. A short time later, the running pheasant scent trail crossed the cat scent trail, and Meika came to an abrupt stop. I encouraged her to stay on the bird, but the sweet smell of cat was more than she could resist. She took a hard turn and headed after the cat. I followed her to a small tree where a big black cat sat staring down at the dog. I literally had to drag Meika away from the tree and the fairly sizable cat—a beast that looked like it could do some damage to a dog if they ever tangled.

Unfortunately, there were at least three neighborhood cats that weren't so lucky.

For the most part, Meika and all of our other dogs over the years stayed in our fenced backyard. I built the fence with my own bare hands, specifically to keep dogs in. For the most part it did a good job. But the fence was not as good at keeping cats out of the yard.

I would have probably done something drastic if Meika was out in the neighborhood killing all of the neighbors' cats, but I didn't feel like it was my duty to keep the wandering cats from coming into our yard. And even though there were some good-sized trees in the backyard where a cat could seek refuge, three different times I found dead cats in the yard.

Another time, as I was getting ready for work, I heard the ungodliest screeching and howling in the backyard. I rushed out the back door and found Meika with a dead ferret in her mouth. We knew the next-door neighbors kept ferrets in their house. What we quickly found out was that one had escaped and picked the wrong yard to explore.

It was during my "Meika years" when I started traveling to other states to do some hunting. She was just a pup and still too young to go when I made my first trip to South Dakota, but over the years she went with me to North Dakota several times.

Meika traveled pretty well, but as I mentioned earlier, she was kind of a one-man dog. So, it shouldn't have surprised me during our motel stays when she would climb up on my bed, lay her head on the pillow next to me, and fall soundly asleep. She never slept on a bed, or on any other furniture for that matter, at our house, so it amazed me when she jumped up on the bed in the motel that first time. It was like she had done it every night of her life, yet it only happened on our trips out of town.

Meika definitely had some other quirks too. One that drove me crazy was her bad habit of running around the neighborhood for fifteen minutes before she would load into the truck to leave for an early morning hunt. I should have had her on a leash, but just when I was thinking I needed to do that, she would run and jump into the back of the truck, literally right out of the gate. Of course, the next time I would have to follow her up and down the block at 5 a.m., prowling around in the various yards, trying to call her name soft enough so the neighbors wouldn't notify the police.

"Bill, what's that noise?"

"Oh, it's just that Phillips idiot running up and down the street, trying hard not to scream his dog's name."

"Do you think we should call the police?"

"Nah, he does it every weekend. He just seems a little more put out this week."

Meika was a bit of a fighter too. Not with other unfamiliar dogs, but with a Lab named Cassie that became part of the Phillips family when Meika was four years old.

Most of the time, Meika and Cassie were the best of friends. They would play together, sleep together, and keep each other company when the rest of the family was away at work and school. But a couple of times, for some reason that never became clear to me, Meika would just tear into poor Cassie.

Cassie was the sweetest dog you have ever seen, very easy going and not looking for any trouble. Maybe it was Meika's way of stating her case for being the alpha, but she would take after Cassie like she wanted to kill her.

When the few battles occurred, it sounded like, well, one heck of a dogfight—which it was. I would run out the back door with a broom and a bucket of water and try to get them separated. Meika would *not* let up. And even though Cassie was so meek and mild, she couldn't just stand there and take it, so she fought back some.

Finally, on about their third or fourth battle, Cassie evidently had had enough. She was younger, stronger, and outweighed Meika by about forty pounds. When I heard the fight start, I grabbed the broom and bucket and headed out the back door to find Cassie on top of Meika. I got them separated, and from that day on, Meika never started another fight with Cassie.

There is a lesson in there for all of us, I think.

Meika had an excellent nose. And as the name of her breed implied, she was a pointer. She'd point whatever we were hunting, if the bird would hold. The pheasants in Central Washington are renowned for their ability to run, which has to be frustrating for a pointing dog. But, especially early in the season, when the birds of the year are still uneducated, they will hold for a point.

Later in the season though, they rarely sit still. Unless, that is, an overnight snowstorm dumps several inches on them when they are roosting. On those days, no matter if it was a Saturday or a Wednesday, a person should plan on calling in sick and getting the dogs out there, because the hunting can be fabulous.

I was able to get Meika out on a couple perfect snowy days during her hunting years, and we had some really fun hunts. She would go on point, I would wade into the snowy brush, and a bird would pop up. Many times, the bird would be a hen, but a few times it would be a big old rooster, and if I did my job, we would get him.

That being said, Meika was not the best retrieving dog I've ever had. In fact, she was probably the worst. Oh, she'd go find a downed bird, but sometimes she would find it, pick it up, drop it, and head off to find another.

One time while hunting in a big asparagus field, I dropped a rooster that you could tell was going to be a runner. His head was up, and his landing gear was down as he crashed into the asparagus bushes. Without a dog, many times those birds get away, only to become a coyote's dinner.

There were a few inches of fresh snow on the ground, so I knew I could probably track the wounded bird if I had to, but I also saw Meika bouncing toward where the bird fell. I walked that way and pretty soon, Meika trotted my direction, but she didn't have the pheasant. As I looked a little closer, I could see some gold and reddish feathers in her mouth. She had found the bird, she even had it in her mouth, but she didn't bring it back.

"Dang it, Meika!" I admonished. "Go get that bird!"

She turned and headed back up the asparagus row. I followed her tracks in the snow, not the way she went but from where she had come. They led me right to the rooster, dead in the snow. Meika was clearly done with that bird and went off looking for a new, much more alive one.

There are proponents of teaching a dog to fetch by forcing it to do so. I thought about this method a time or two after crawling through some brush to pick up a bird that I knew Meika had already found. But just when I had cussed her for not retrieving a pheasant or quail to me, she would bring one back just as pretty as you please.

She knew how to retrieve, and when she did, I would praise her to no end, but it wasn't a priority for her. I learned quickly to keep an eye on where any bird I shot fell, because even though Meika was headed that way, I still might need to go pick up the bird. It was definitely hit and miss with her, and it was a vexing little quirk that I just learned to live with.

After all, she was still one heck of a pointer. In the hundreds of points I had with Meika over the years, a couple come to mind. One happened on a wintry morning when we were on a late-season pheasant hunt. We were working some heavy cattails along some ponds. Pheasants love to dig down into cattails when it gets snowy and cold. It's good thermal cover, and if you can find a big cattail patch near a food source, it can be a real pheasant magnet.

Meika was working the edge of a long line of cattails between a dyke and a pond. When she went on point, I figured she had a pheasant nailed down. I started to walk down to the edge of the cattails next to Meika when up jumped a mallard drake. I don't know why it surprised me so much to see a duck get up, but I almost didn't shoot. Almost. I dropped the drake in the pond, and as if she knew this was an exceptional moment, Meika swam out there, picked up the duck, and delivered it to my hand like a retrieving champion.

Of course, she was a pointer, and the duck was holding in the cattails, so I shouldn't have been surprised by the point. It was the only time she pointed a duck, but not the last time she retrieved one.

Another point that stands out took place in North Dakota.

A group of friends from Yakima and I had headed to Mott, North Dakota to hunt on a ranch that, at the time, had thousands of wild pheasants. Coming from an area with far fewer pheasants, it felt to us like pheasant nirvana.

At the time, Meika was in her prime. She was a pheasant-hunting machine, and when she landed in North Dakota, she must have thought she had died and gone to heaven.

On the last day of our three-day hunt, four of us were spread out and working through some prairie grass that wasn't quite heavy or thick enough to hold the birds. As we walked, I kept looking well ahead of us and watched as dozens of birds flushed out of the field.

Since there were so many birds around, I probably could have just stayed with the group, and we would have eventually gotten into more birds. But I had learned at an early age that if the birds are getting up out of range, you need to get your butt up there as fast as you can. So, I took off running in a wide circle to try to get ahead of the running, flushing pheasants.

My dogs learn quickly that if I take off running, they need to as well, and Meika ran alongside me on the sprint up a gradual hill to the end of the grass. When we got there, me out of breath and Meika ready to hunt, she immediately got on a hot scent and went on point. A rooster jumped up, and somehow between gasps for oxygen, I busted him.

Meika went to get the rooster, but on her way, she went on point again. The pheasant I had just shot was my third and final bird of the day, so I waved at the other guys to get up to where we were.

Two of the three guys hustled up the hill, but it still took them a couple of minutes. The whole time Meika just stood there, frozen in a beautiful point. When the guys finally arrived, I told them to walk past the dog and just keep walking in the direction she was pointing. They did, and fifteen yards ahead, they jumped a rooster and dropped it.

Now, most of you pointing-dog folks out there have probably had dogs hold points for much longer than that, but it was Meika's longest point. I can still picture her, locked solid, nose into the breeze that riffled her beautiful brown feathery coat, with the sun shining down through the white puffy clouds of the blue North Dakota sky.

We found both roosters and then we all sat down for a drink of water and a rest. I don't know if Meika actually thought it was heaven, but I thought it was mighty close.

Chapter 6

*"Dogs have a way of finding the people who need them
and filling an emptiness we didn't ever know we had."*
                                                    –Thom Jones

Most dogs go like gangbusters when you start hunting a field, but many, especially the older dogs, figure out that when the group gets together and heads toward the trucks, the hunt is over for now.

Meika was not one of those dogs. She would hunt every step of the way back to the truck, even if we were crossing a dirt field or walking through cover so short it wouldn't hide a hummingbird. That didn't matter to her. She was out there to hunt, dammit, and that was what she was going to do.

The problem with this trait had more to do with her human hunting partner. You would think I would have learned to pay attention to Meika all the way back to the truck, no matter what type of cover we were walking in. But that's not what happened.

I recall one brisk fall morning when a group of four or five of us was walking down a dirt road back to the trucks. It was probably only a half-mile walk, and we were all laughing and talking, guns over our shoulders as we hiked.

Occasionally, I would check on Meika. She was nearby, but she was still hunting. She wasn't acting birdy at all, and the grass she was hunting looked like it wouldn't hold anything bigger than a mouse, let alone a rooster pheasant. So, stupidly, I ignored her.

When the rooster pheasant jumped up just in front of Meika, not fifteen yards away, it scared all of us. The big, beautiful bird even cackled as it made its escape, laughing at us. Nobody got a shot off, as most of us, for safety reasons, had unloaded our shotguns. The ones who still had a shell in their guns were either too flabbergasted to shoot or had people in their way.

Meika did this several times in her hunting career. Although I wasn't always paying attention to her, I learned fairly quickly that I needed to keep an eye on her at all times, because you just never knew when she was going to go on point or put up a bird.

Not that she cared, but Meika was actually a TV star. At least for thirty minutes.

One day I was chatting with Scott Linden, a prolific outdoor writer and dog lover from Oregon, who told me he was putting together a TV show for one of the outdoor networks that featured different types of hunting dogs.

At some point in an earlier conversation, I had told Scott about my German longhaired pointer, and he remembered that. Eventually, he asked if I, along with said pointer, would like to appear on his show.

Throughout my years as an outdoor writer, and in my promotional work with Yakima Bait Company, I have appeared on a variety of fishing TV shows. So, doing a hunting show sounded like fun. The show was called, *What the Dogs Taught Me*, and Scott had it set up for us to hunt for some pen-raised birds in Ellensburg.

Meika didn't care if it was pen-raised, Mother Nature-raised, or really, if it was even a bird. She hunted anything. I mentioned the cats. I'm sure she would have hunted rabbits if that was what we were going to hunt that day.

Scott, who hunts today with wirehaired pointing griffons, was pretty interested in Meika and her breed. And although Meika was getting up there in age, she hunted hard and she found the planted birds.

If I remember correctly, it was a very windy day, which is normal for the Kittitas Valley, making the scenting conditions difficult and the shooting challenging.

It was a fun day of hunting with Scott, who is very knowledgeable about dogs and other outdoorsy things. His most recent TV show is called *Wingshooting USA*. None of my motley crew of Labrador retrievers, or I, have been invited to participate in that show. Meika was definitely the reason for the invite all those many years ago. It was her fifteen, or more correctly, thirty minutes of fame.

Anyone who has ever hunted with a longhaired dog understands how different they are from short-haired dogs. I had never given it much thought until the first day I hunted in Central Washington with Meika.

My Labs would never need much grooming after a hunt. I would routinely check them for any cuts or stickers in their pads. From time to time, they would need their eyes flushed of seeds and debris, but other than that, they were pretty maintenance free.

Meika, like other longhaired breeds, I'm sure, was a cocklebur magnet. The clingy seeds, about the size of a grape, would get into her long hair and migrate inward, knotting up more fur and hair, until they were hopelessly stuck.

Many a Saturday evening, after a long day in the field, the first thing we would do at home was lay out an old sheet, set Meika on it, and go to work on the burrs in her hair. Or more correctly, she would use her teeth to pull the ones she could reach, and I would pull or cut out the rest of them. These little burr-pulling sessions would last for an hour or more, and sometimes Meika would be so tired from running miles and miles during the day, she'd just lie there and let me work on her. Eyes closed, she would try to sleep as I pulled and clipped. Once in a while she would whimper, especially if the burr I was working on was up against skin, but most of the time she would lie there and let it happen.

Pulling burrs can be tough on the puller too. Every cocklebur has hundreds of prickly little spines, with a tiny sharp hook on each end, and they would easily stick fingers too. The next day or two after working on getting the burrs out of Meika, if I was trying to do anything with my hands, my fingertips would burn with pain.

I actually started purposefully avoiding hunting some fields where I knew the cockleburs were bad. But inevitably, Meika would somehow find a patch of the ornery burrs during a day's hunt, and we would end up on the living room floor that evening.

During the hunt, after each field, I would check Meika for burrs, especially under her legs, where the pesky things could literally scratch and irritate her skin until it bled.

It wasn't just the cockleburs that would end up in Meika's coat. There are all kinds of other seeds out there that are spread by clinging to animals (and hunters) as they brush past. By the end of our burr-picking sessions, I would have a pile of all kinds of noxious little stickers and seeds.

At this point, some of you might be wondering why I didn't just give Meika a haircut. Believe me, I thought about that after the second time we did the whole burr-picking routine.

I went to the local pet store and bought some clippers, fully intending to give Meika a nice haircut. What is the saying about best laid plans? I wish I would have made a video of my little brown pup when I tried to give her a haircut. She cowered and shivered at just the sound of the clippers, then ran and hid when I tried to touch her with them. She absolutely hated them.

After fighting her to stand still and let me work on her several times, I finally threw up my hands and told her, "Fine, we'll just pick the burrs."

Somehow, she seemed to know what I was telling her, because she immediately stopped quivering and licked my face.

The clippers went into the drawer, never to see the light of day again, and Meika and I picked about a million more burrs during the remainder of her hunting days. Some days there would only be a few, and others there would be fifty or sixty or more.

We still have the dog clippers, although I'm not sure why. All the dogs that came into our life after Meika have been short-haired Labs. Whenever I see the clippers, I am reminded of Meika and the hours we spent picking burrs.

Meika was a hard hunter all her life—which was a long one. She lived sixteen years and hunted until she was thirteen. Finally, tired bones, sore joints, bad hearing, and failing eyesight were too much to overcome in the field. But she never lost the desire to go hunting.

It was hard to watch her grow old, but she seemed to enjoy retirement, sleeping on her favorite pillow or out in the sun under the willow tree.

On occasion she would get up and do a perimeter check of the backyard. She would sniff here and there, searching for who knows what. Other than a rare stray cat, and the neighbors ferret that once, nothing ever entered the backyard that could be taken as interesting, much less dangerous.

Of course, a herd of hippos could have stomped through the backyard while she was sleeping, and Meika wouldn't have heard it. Sometimes she slept so soundly through noises and commotion that a bystander, unaware of the situation, would conclude that the brown dog was dead. I even thought that a time or two. But a closer look at her petite little frame would show her ribs rising and falling.

In those last few years she developed a funny but annoying habit that I never quite understood. After she had done her perimeter check and deemed the area all clear of intruders, Meika would oftentimes walk right to the dead center of the yard, stick her nose up in the air, and start barking. Obviously, she'd smelled something that needed to be barked at, but why do it sitting in the middle of the yard?

When she was younger and could hear, I would go to the back window when Meika started barking and just tap on it. She would stop, and that would be that. The loss of hearing made the window-tapping useless, so to get her to quit, I would have to go out and get into her line of sight, then shake a finger at her. Otherwise, she had no idea she was being scolded.

Occasionally, during her marathon retirement naps, Meika's legs would twitch and jerk. And she would even yip and growl. Dog dreams, I assumed. Hopefully, she was dreaming of days in the field, trying to corner a crafty rooster pheasant or working to pin down a covey of quail.

Meika lived longer than any dog that has been part of my life, either before or after. She was a tough old bird. Fit as a fiddle. Other than a kidney infection and a uterine infection, she stayed in perfect health. That is if you don't include the hearing and seeing issues in her last few years.

None of my dogs have ever liked being retired. After years of seeing the boots and shotgun come out, and knowing they were going to go do the thing they loved best in the whole wide world, to have to be left at home had to be difficult for them.

I knew it was time to retire Meika when, in the fall of her

fourteenth year, I took her out to one of our favorite haunts, and she just couldn't get through the thick brush. Within minutes she was walking on my heels.

After that, she would raise a fuss when I grabbed our young Lab to go hunting, but she knew she couldn't do it anymore. Usually, within minutes of us leaving, Terri said Meika would be back curled up in the sun under the willow tree, dreaming, hopefully of the good old days when younger legs, better hearing, and good vision had her doing what she loved most: running through the fall fields, looking for one more rooster pheasant to point.

I have always contended that dogs, or should I say most dogs, are way smarter than most of us think. And they have an uncanny way of communicating.

Terri, the boys, and I had been out to a family dinner, and when we got home about 8:30 p.m. one evening, I looked out into the backyard and didn't see the dogs. Meika and our young Lab, Cassie, would almost always be at the back window when we got home, because they knew I would let them in, or at least come say hi and give them a small treat.

On this evening, I looked out the back window and only saw Cassie, who was bouncing up and down on her back legs.

"That's weird," I said to Terri. "I wonder where Meika is." I went to the back door, and Cassie was there, still bouncing. Then she ran to the water dish and back to the door.

"What is it, girl?" I asked the big black dog.

She turned and ran to the dog dish again. I followed her.

Meika was next to the dish in serious distress. In an instant, I knew she'd had a stroke. All I could think of was how we needed to get her to a vet and help her out of her misery.

This was before our town had a twenty-four-hour emergency vet clinic, so I had to call my vet. His service put me in touch with the veterinarian who was on call.

When I finally was able to reach the vet and told her what our situation was, she said, "Ugh, I just got home."

If I could have reached through the phone and grabbed that woman, I would have done so in an instant. Then I would have shaken her for a bit. Instead, I said, "Ma'am, my dog is in bad shape. She needs to be put down. What would you like me to do?"

Her words said she would come back to her office, but the sound of her voice and the attitude coming through the phone said it was the last thing in the world she wanted to do.

I said, "Ma'am, I understand you've put in a long day, but my dog is suffering, and I can't let her spend the night like this."

The very unhappy vet met me at my car in the parking lot of her clinic. Without moving Meika into the clinic, she administered the medication that relieved my little hunting partner of her pain. I handed the vet a wad of cash. Then, bawling like a baby with Meika still in the back of the rig, I drove home, swearing I would never take an animal to that woman again, even if she was the last vet in the state.

Luckily, I've never had to. The veterinarians I've used before and since have all been caring people. They understand that our animals are as much a part of our families as our children. I am sure that vet had had a bad day, but that experience taught me a lesson about how to treat people, and animals, no matter how badly the day has gone.

As with the previous dogs in my adult life, I buried Meika, with the help of Kyle, the next day in one of the fields we hunted together for more than a decade. Every time I drive by that spot, and whenever I hunt some of the fields that Meika liked to hunt, cockleburs and all, I remember the little dog that I didn't know I wanted.

Chapter 7

"Whoever said you can't buy happiness forgot little puppies."

–Gene Hill

Picking out a puppy is always a bit of a challenge. I liken it to the famous line from the movie *Forrest Gump*. A litter of whining, wiggling, beautiful puppies is like a box of chocolates. You never know what you're gonna get.

Buying a puppy sight unseen, without seeing the parents or really knowing the hunting background of the sire and dam, makes it even more of a gamble. But that is exactly what I did with my next dog.

While at a fishing tackle show one summer, I was talking to a friend who worked as a sales representative for one of the big fishing hook manufacturers in the Portland, Oregon area. One thing led to another and pretty soon, we were talking about hunting dogs. It so happened that this gentleman had a litter of black Lab puppies on the way, and when he found out that I was in the market for a new pup, we struck a deal. He owned the dam, which was not registered, and because the puppies couldn't be papered, he was going to sell them for fifty dollars.

If you watch the internet like I do, you know that there is no such thing as a "cheap" hunting dog anymore. Most of the recognized breeds now sell for several hundreds of dollars, with some selling for a thousand bucks or more.

Even back then, it was hard to find a fifty-dollar hunting dog. Especially a "purebred" dog.

Never being one to pass up a deal, especially after hearing

that both parents were hunters, I told the acquaintance I would definitely be interested in one of the pups. Having a registered dog never meant much to me, mostly because I wasn't wanting to run them in any hunt tests, and I definitely wasn't interested in raising any puppies.

One of my hunting buddies was also interested, as it turned out. I had told my good friend Merle Shuyler about the pups, and he happened to be thinking about getting a new hunting dog. So, I called the sales rep and reserved one of the pups for him as well. Merle also likes a good deal, and the fifty-dollar price tag was especially enticing to him.

A couple months later, the gentleman called and said the pups were ready to go to their new homes. I jumped in the car and headed to Portland, where I met him in the parking lot of a mini-mart just off the freeway, and we made the exchange. Just like a shady drug deal, I gave him a crisp new Benjamin Franklin, and he handed over a box with two jet-black Lab puppies in it.

As is the case with every other eight-week-old puppy in the world, the two little black balls of fur were incredibly cute. With their big beautiful brown eyes, they stole my heart. It was going to be hard to pick one out of the pair of sisters.

Talk to five different people about how to pick out a pup, and each one will have a different opinion on the subject. Again, you never really know with pups of that age. They can be meek and mild or overly aggressive. Some will follow a pheasant wing, others won't. If they have the hunting gene, hopefully it will pop up at some point, and you'll have a good hunting partner for the next decade or more.

I don't remember now how I ended up settling on the pup we named Cassie. I probably just flipped a coin. Merle took the other pup and named her Maggie. In the end, we were both happy with the pups we got.

Cassie grew quickly, and as she did, some questions about her lineage began to creep up. Yes, she was all black, but her ears were slightly smaller than what you would see on a full-blooded Lab. And they had a funny fold in them. Just not quite Lab-like. Then there was her fur. She had short hair, but also a coat of fluffy under-hair that would shed at the weirdest times. The fur had the feel of the fur from a German shepherd or some other dog.

Merle's dog, Maggie, while not quite as big, had some of the same non-Lab traits as Cassie.

Even with the unknown background in her breeding, or the breeding of her parents or grandparents, Cassie was a pretty good hunter. Never the swiftest runner of the dogs I've had, Cassie would just plod along, enjoying her time in the field, looking for whatever it was we were hunting.

It is always hard to tell what kind of nose a dog has. I've seen the best hunting dogs, with supposedly great noses, run right over the top of a holding pheasant. While another dog, without the same pedigree, might find the bird that the champion missed. That was Cassie. She couldn't or didn't want to keep up with the other dogs in the field, but there were dozens of times she would work along at her own pace and flush a bird all the other, faster dogs had missed.

She would also find and retrieve birds that none of the other dogs could locate.

I remember one particular pheasant Cassie found for me that I am positive I never would have put in the bag if it weren't for her plodding diligence.

Which dog flushed the pheasant, I can't remember, but I can still see the big rooster breaking over the top of some brush and trees. I shot, and the bird went down, but I couldn't see exactly where. As is usually the case when we hunt with a group of people and dogs, the sound of the shot almost always attracts all the four-legged members of our team. They come to look for whatever might have fallen from the sky.

Several dogs were swirling around, nose to the ground, looking for the rooster when I came around the brush. I couldn't find Cassie. Knowing that she sometimes would work out the downed-bird puzzle in her slow, methodical way, I wondered if she might have the wounded rooster on the run.

I looked around and finally saw Cassie's butt and tail sticking out from under a huge pile of brush. When I got over there, I could see her trying to back out of the brush. But every time she worked out a few inches, she'd be pulled back in.

When I got close enough to look into the pile, I could see that Cassie had the rooster by its head, but he was still very much alive. In fact, he was alive enough to be backpedaling with enough strength to keep dragging the big dog into the brush pile.

Most Labs have a soft mouth, meaning they will not bite into a downed bird. Cassie had a very soft mouth, and in this case, it was detrimental to her making the retrieve. She wouldn't let go of the rooster's head, but she also wouldn't bite into it, which would have killed the bird and put a stop to the game of tug-of-war.

I watched Cassie keep working and working on getting the rooster out of the brush. Finally, she pulled it out far enough that I could get to the bird and put it out of its misery. With the bird dead, I gave it back to Cassie, and she pranced around with the rooster in her mouth with a pride that only hunters see. Her funny-shaped ears were back. She walked around, head held high, showing the rooster to the other dogs as if to say, "See what I did while you were all running around like wild animals?"

It took me a while to learn to pay attention to Cassie. She started her career hunting with Meika, who was hell on wheels with an athletic build and stamina that allowed her to cover the field like a wide receiver. Cassie was more like a big, old lineman, doing her job in a steady, workman-like way.

It was natural to think that because Meika was normally ten steps or more ahead of Cassie, the brown dog with the long hair was on the bird. She might have been on *a* bird, but Cassie would often pick up another bird. Some dogs look "birdy" all the time. When Cassie had her nose to the ground, and her tail was whirling like a helicopter, she was definitely birdy. When you saw that, you could count on something to flush very soon.

While I hunted upland birds a lot with my dogs back in those days, my hunting buddies and I also did a fair amount of duck hunting. One of our favorite hunts was to run down to the Columbia River and haul a few dozen decoys to the shoreline on the Umatilla National Wildlife Refuge. We would set them out in the river, build a tumbleweed blind, and wait for the waterfowl to return from feeding in the nearby fields.

Cassie enjoyed retrieving ducks, and being mostly Lab, she loved the water. Sometimes, though, a duck falling into the Columbia, especially one that was only winged, would just be too much for her. I hated losing those occasional ducks, but when it looked like the bird was getting too far out into the huge river, I would call her back.

On one of our trips down to the Columbia, we were all set up to hunt when a man and his son came in about three hundred yards downriver of us. They started setting out their decoys, and right from the start, the man started yelling at the boy.

"I told you to move that decoy to the left!" the man would scream at the top of his lungs. Constantly berating the boy got old very quickly. After listening to it for long enough, we started making snide comments, loudly.

"Gee, Dad, it sure is fun hunting with you!" one of us would yell. "Can we go again next weekend?"

It seemed to work, and the man stopped yelling at the poor kid. I can't imagine what home life was like for the boy, and his siblings, and probably mother. The guy came off as an A-1 asshole.

Finally, after the yelling stopped, the ducks started flying. The man and the boy, as well as our group of guys, got some shooting in.

We watched as the man's black Lab streaked into the river and swam to retrieve, sometimes even on birds that were way out there. I was impressed, though I'm sure he was as strict with the dog as he was with the boy.

Anyway, a group of mallards dropped into our decoys, and one of us shot a nice big drake that flapped quite a good distance before folding out in the river. Cassie started after the downed duck, but I knew immediately she wouldn't make it, so I called her back.

Evidently, the man had watched this, and when the duck floated by in front of them—maybe two hundred yards from shore—he sent his dog out after it.

Again, I was impressed. We watched as the dog fought the current and got to the duck, then turned and swam back. The man took the duck from the dog's mouth and started walking toward our blind.

"Oh crap," I said to my partners. "One of you has to go face that guy and get your duck."

There was a quick chorus of "I didn't shoot that duck."

Finally, one of my buddies worked up the courage to walk down and meet the guy halfway. My buddy told the guy he had a great dog and thanked him for having the Lab retrieve the bird.

No other words were exchanged, but the guy never yelled at the boy the rest of the day, so maybe our comments made a tiny difference.

I know I learned something from the experience. I told myself I would never treat my sons that way, or anyone else for that matter.

It was on another one of our duck hunts to the Columbia that Cassie pulled a funny one.

My longtime friend Doug Jewett, his son Brandon, my son Kyle, and I all headed to the same area on the Columbia near Paterson to hunt waterfowl. I don't remember shooting many ducks that day, but I do remember how, during a lull in the morning, Meika and Cassie slipped away to explore the surroundings.

Again, I'm by no means a dog trainer. Because I hunted mostly upland birds, my dogs had a tough time sitting in a blind where they could see almost nothing of what was going on. They would pile out of the blind, and sometimes through it, when we stood to shoot. There was no sitting patiently until they were told to go fetch. As long as they didn't break someone's leg leaving the blind, and went to retrieve the ducks, I was okay with it.

Out of boredom, I assume, the two dogs went on a bit of a walkabout. I didn't worry about them because they never went far, and soon they wandered back over to the blinds. For some reason, Cassie decided to go sit in Doug and Brandon's blind. They didn't have a dog at that time, so I had no problem with Cassie sitting with them.

A few seconds after Cassie plopped down in their blind, I heard Doug start gagging and choking.

"What's the matter?" I called from our blind.

"Cassie rolled in something and stinks like a dead fish!" Doug coughed.

Doug undersold the smell just a tad. Cassie smelled like dead, rotting fish that had been sitting in the sun for weeks after a skunk had sprayed it. The stench was horrible. Why she decided to sit in the Jewetts' blind after she'd anointed herself with the ghastly smell is still a mystery. I guess she figured Doug wouldn't holler at another man's dog.

If I remember right, it took several weeks before the fishy smell was totally gone from Cassie. Doug later reported to me he had to throw away the gloves he was wearing when he petted her.

Speaking of breaking someone's leg, Cassie almost broke one of my legs on a pheasant hunt.

During the 1990s, the Yakima Valley was a big producer of asparagus. After the last cutting of the tasty little spears each spring, the farmers would let the next bunch of spears grow until they reached about three feet in height and started producing little red berries. The asparagus would get big and bushy at the top, and with thousands of them planted in neat, long rows, the asparagus fields quickly became popular loafing and feeding spots for pheasants.

The Schilperoort family was a big grower of asparagus in the lower Yakima Valley, and they were always very nice to let our rag-tag bunch of hunters and dogs hunt the asparagus fields that had gone to seed in the fall.

Hunting the fields was challenging, for sure. Hunters worked along the rows, but because the asparagus was so bushy and thick, you couldn't see what was going on at ground level. The pheasants, which always prefer running to flying, would run circles around us as we walked, or they would run to the end of the field and fly.

We almost always had some hunters posted at the end of the field to try and stop the escaping pheasants. And we counted on the dogs to keep working ahead of us to flush the birds that were trying to double back.

As you walked, you could hear the dogs running back and forth, and you'd occasionally see one pop up to check on the hunters. If a bird got up in the middle of the field, it was a good bet there was a dog right on its tail.

It was during one of these hunts that Cassie about killed me. As was usual for us when we hunted the asparagus, I was one of the walkers because I had dogs, and they would hunt with me working the birds toward the end of the field.

I can't remember why I started running down field, but I did. Probably because I saw a bunch of pheasants getting up and thought if I could get twenty yards closer quickly, I might get a shot.

It was a fool's errand for a couple reasons. First, I am what some people might call a klutz. I prefer to think otherwise, but we'll not argue that point here. The other reason was that running anywhere when you literally can't see your own two feet is not very smart.

Being clumsy and stupid never stopped me before, so off I went. What I hadn't factored into the equation was Cassie.

All my dogs learn quickly that there is a reason to run when I take off running. Usually, it means I have seen a bird that they have yet to detect, and so they will start running beside me or ahead of me.

On this day, Cassie figured out I was sprinting down the asparagus rows, and for some reason, she decided she needed to be in the exact row I was in. The big dog crossed over to my lane and hit me in mid-stride. She knocked me so hard that I did a flip, landing on my back. Luckily, I crash-landed in the soft dirt of an asparagus mound. I swear that I couldn't have been hit any harder by an NFL linebacker.

Evidently, my flight through the asparagus field was quite a sight. It provided a rousing chuckle for those who witnessed it.

As I lay there, making sure I had not dislocated any knees or ankles, Cassie came to check that I was okay. She sat next to me and licked my cheek. It was her way of saying she was sorry, and of making sure I was okay.

Cassie, while big and not terribly fleet of foot, certainly wasn't stupid. One little trick she learned quickly was to keep an eye on Meika, my older hunting dog at the time.

Hunting with more than one dog can be challenging. You need to watch both of them at the same time, which is close to impossible. One dog can be over here and get on a bird, while the other dog is over there, possibly on a different bird.

Over the years when the two dogs hunted together, Cassie would actually let me know that Meika was on a bird. Yes, Cassie would hunt on her own, but the second she saw Meika either start working a bird or go on point, the big black dog would rush to where Meika was.

Now, there's no need to send me any harsh emails about hunting a flushing dog with a pointing dog. This was a long time ago, and Meika was the only true pointing dog I ever had. So, there was no keeping Cassie by my side until I walked in on the flush like you see on the bird hunting shows on TV.

Thus, it was up to me to try to keep an eye on both dogs, and when Cassie started making a beeline for Meika, I needed to hustle that way too. Inevitably, there would be a bird on the end of the sprint.

I would have liked to know how Meika felt about Cassie crashing her pointing party. She did all the work, and Cassie got the glory of flushing the bird. But she seemed to put up with it. When it was all said and done, Meika would just shrug her shoulders and head off to find another bird to point. And Cassie would go her own way too, but she always knew where her German longhaired sister was, and what she was up to.

Even though there may have been some other breed mixed in, Cassie had all the other Lab traits. She was the sweetest, most loving dog. She absolutely loved to be petted and would come over and put her big head in my lap. She loved to eat, but she would gladly give up her meal if it meant she could get some lovings from one of her people.

I ended up retiring Cassie when she was about nine years old. She had arthritis in her back hips that kept her from running very well, or for very long. Other than that, though, she was an amazing dog considering the maladies some of my other dogs had to deal with. She rarely went to the vet other than to get her vaccinations and to be spayed. Overall, Cassie was an easy dog to have and totally worry free.

If there is such a thing, Cassie was the quintessential fifty-dollar dog: a Labrador retriever of questionable heritage, purchased sight unseen. All in all, she was an excellent investment and a fond member of our family for fourteen years.

To this day, I've never owned a dog that has died of natural causes. When I have lost a dog, it has always been because they needed to be put down. Over the years I've had to do it too many times. Though never an easy thing to do, the first three times were made slightly less difficult by the fact that the dogs were suffering from cancer or a stroke. But making a life-and-death decision when the dog is still of fairly sound mind is a real heartbreaker.

Cassie had been failing for some time. She had lost some teeth, and the ones she still had were worn with age, making chewing difficult. Her back legs were arthritic, making it hard for her to stand up or stay standing for any length of time. And her breathing was often strained, especially during hot summer days.

Then came the issues with bladder and bowel control.

Even with these physical problems, Cassie was still happy to greet me. And although it tested her patience to no end, she even seemed to enjoy the frolicking and camaraderie of the younger Lab I had introduced into the family.

When it became clear that the happiest, friendliest dog in the world was no longer happy, I knew it was time. Her tail wagged very infrequently, and when you looked into her big brown eyes, you could see that she just wasn't enjoying life. She didn't seem to be in pain, but when she would fall and struggle to get up, or when she would have to lie down to finish her dinner, I knew the time was near.

The final motivation to help end any potential suffering was remembering the previous summer when Cassie had been struggling so much in the heat. With the control of her bodily functions failing, along with the progression of her other physical ailments, I decided she shouldn't have to endure any more hot Central Washington days.

The visit to the vet's office was quick and painless. And as soon as Cassie was gone, I knew it was the right decision. She was in a better place, and it no longer mattered that her legs, lungs, and other body parts weren't working very well.

Later, as we took one final drive to one of our favorite pheasant hunting fields, Kyle and I reminisced about the many hunts we'd shared with Cassie over the years. And as we dug her grave under the shade of a tree, we laughed and cried, remembering Cassie and her life with us.

There were many pheasant and duck hunts that included uncountable flushes and finds and retrieves. But there were other times when Cassie was, well, just Cassie. She wasn't the best hunting dog I've ever had, but she wasn't bad either. I could have done a lot worse. And as far as a companion and just a big, sweet dog goes, there were none better. When I bought Cassie for fifty dollars, I had no idea what I was getting. In the end, it was the best fifty dollars I ever spent.

Chapter 8

"A dog is the only thing on earth that loves you more than he loves himself."

—Josh Billings

About the time Cassie was slowing down, I started searching for my next hunting dog. As it turned out, I didn't have to look far.

My sister Diane and her husband Jim Dunn had a nice black Lab named Lacey. She was a good little hunter, and Jim and Di decided they would like to have a pup from her, so they called me to see if I knew anyone with a registered male Lab that might make for a good breeding partner with their dog.

One of the guys I hunted with frequently, Mike Schell, had a hard-hunting yellow Lab named Jake. So, I put my sister in touch with Mike.

Well, one thing led to another and a few months later, Lacey had a litter of nine pups. When the pups were eight weeks old, Mike, our friend Merle Shuyler, and I all went down to pick out our pups.

Mike, who got the pick of the litter as his payment for Jake's stud service, took a plump little black male, and I got to pick my pup next. Again, you never know what you are going to get, but I took a shining to one little female that was almost white.

Merle also took a female, but one that was more gold in color. Over the years the three siblings would hunt together often, and all were fine bird dogs.

The little white pup that we named Sierra took to me almost immediately, and from day one she was the nicest, sweetest little dog. She never cried or even whined once when she left her mama and litter-mates. It was as if she knew that wherever I was, she was supposed to be there too. She didn't cry at night or when she was left alone, and she immediately made friends with Cassie, which certainly helped.

More white than yellow, Sierra truly was a Labrador retriever—the retrieving-est retriever I have ever owned. If the wind blew my hat off, Sierra would retrieve it. If I dropped a leather glove somewhere, I didn't have to worry about having to find it, because Sierra invariably would come up behind me with the glove in her mouth.

At dinner time each night, which was probably Sierra's favorite time of day, she would retrieve not only her dish, but all of the other dog dishes that somehow got distributed around the yard during the twenty-four hours since the last feeding. In fact, if you inadvertently forgot that it was time to feed the poor, starving dogs, Sierra would take it upon herself to retrieve a dish. She would sit, hold it in her mouth, and stare at the back window so that anyone who might look out in the yard would know it was dinnertime.

And while she liked to retrieve balls, throwing dummies, sticks, rocks, hats, and dog dishes, Sierra *loved* to retrieve birds. She was a pheasant, dove, quail, chukar, and duck-retrieving fool.

Sierra came into my life around the time that antler hunting was really taking off. After reading articles about teaching dogs to find shed antlers, I realized if there was ever a dog that could become an antler hunter, Sierra was it. The author of the article wrote that shed-hunting dogs need to be trained specifically for such a duty. And he said that antler-seeking dogs should not be regular hunting dogs. That made sense too.

The thought of having a dog out with me if I ever really got into shed hunting intrigued me. It was the whole bird hunting versus shed antler hunting conundrum that eventually got me. Sierra loved to hunt birds so much, and I didn't really care about trying to find some sheds out amongst the legion of antler hunters, so I never pursued it. But to this day I wonder just how Sierra might have done. My guess is she would have been great.

While all my dogs have been good hunters and great family dogs, each of them has had a unique personality, including some quirks. One of Sierra's funny oddities was she didn't sleep much. Now, they say (whoever "they" are) that dogs will sleep some twenty hours a day. Not Sierra. In fact, when she was a pup, I rarely saw her sleeping. Not that I was around her all the time, because I was away at work eight to ten hours a day during the week. But even if I'd slip home for lunch and look out into the backyard, Sierra would be awake.

I hadn't paid much attention to it at first, but it seemed like anytime I looked out in the backyard, Sierra was awake while my other two dogs were stretched out in the sun, sound asleep. Sierra would be lying with the other two dogs, but instead of sleeping she would be engaged in any number of activities—most of which involved chewing. From chewing a willow limb, to watching an airplane or a flock of geese fly over, to chewing a piece of garden hose, to chewing a leg of the picnic table, Sierra would be wide awake doing something.

I realize that Sierra was young and my other two dogs were past their prime. But if I remember correctly, the other two had always been able to sleep the day away. I mean, "they" say that's what dogs do.

I even tried one time to see if Sierra did any sleeping when she was in her doghouse. It was one rainy Saturday afternoon and all the dogs were out of sight, which usually meant they were snoozing away in their individual, straw-filled houses. So, I quietly made my way out the back door and slowly peeked into Sierra's house. There she was, just as content as can be, chewing away on her dog dish.

Her constant happiness amazed me. If I never slept, I would be crankier than an old rain-soaked rooster. But no matter what time of day or night, Sierra was just glad to be alive.

I do think she got bored at times, and I often witnessed her grab something and try to entice one of the older dogs into a game of chase or tug-of-war. She would pick up some old stick and prance in front of the sleeping dogs as if to say, "Look what I have. I have a stick, and you can't have it!"

Of course, the older dogs almost always ignored her when she started into this "look what I have" game. But occasionally they would take the bait and off they'd go, romping around the yard, sounding like a herd of stampeding buffalo. Then, once the game was over, the other two older dogs would crash, while Sierra contentedly chewed on whatever the item was that she had used to entice the others into playing.

Even in the warmth of the house, Sierra found it hard to sleep. I remember one night when I brought all three dogs in for the evening. The older dogs quickly found cozy spots to lie down and snooze. Sierra, on the other hand, was like a four-year-old kid that you are trying to get down for a nap.

I would tell her to lie down, which she would do. She would even close her eyes, but after about ten seconds, her thick white Lab tail would start to pound the floor, and up she would be. I'd tell her to lie down again. Then, in a few seconds she would wiggle this way and waggle that way, as if sleeping on the plush front-room carpet was just too comfortable for her.

Finally, after fifteen minutes of squirming and squiggling, I'd often give her a chew bone and send her outside. There, she would find a very comfortable spot on the hard concrete patio and chew to her heart's content.

I was even amazed to see how Sierra couldn't or wouldn't sleep after a hard day of hunting during the fall. After spending all day running through acres and acres of asparagus fields, the two older dogs would pass out in their houses. But Sierra was happy to just lie under the willow tree and watch the world go by, often chewing on whatever was handy. Sierra did do a little more sleeping as she got older, but she was one unique dog that never seemed to want or need to sleep as much as the others.

How does the old adage go? Let sleeping dogs lie. I never really had to worry about that with Sierra.

I always wanted to have one of those real expensive hunting dogs. You know the kind. One that comes with a pedigree as long as Shaquille O'Neal's leg. One that will take hand signals and whistle commands and sit patiently at your side no matter how stressful the situation. One that all your hunting buddies admire and secretly wish they had. One that does everything but call the ducks for you.

Sierra quickly became one of those very expensive dogs, but for very different reasons. She never learned hand signals because I didn't try to teach her, and while she would come to a whistle, that was the extent of her whistle training. Sitting still was another issue. If we stopped walking in the pheasant field for even one minute, she would begin wiggling and squiggling, wanting to get going again. Sitting patiently was not in Sierra's repertoire.

But expensive she was.

First, you need to consider Sierra's purchase price, which was actually pretty reasonable. She was an AKC-registered yellow Lab, and I got her, literally, for a brother-in-law deal of one hundred dollars. At the time, most registered Labs with hunting pedigrees were going for a minimum of three hundred bucks.

The purchase price was just the beginning, however.

Whenever you get a new puppy, you want to get them to the veterinarian for a checkup and all the normal vaccinations. I did that with Sierra. That was seventy-five dollars well spent.

A short time later, when she was nine or ten weeks old, Sierra decided that eating a willow branch would be a fun thing to do. Unfortunately, eating a willow branch was much easier than passing a willow branch.

I don't know how I noticed it, but I looked out into the backyard one Sunday afternoon, and the little white pup was squatting to poop. No biggie. Happened all the time. But when I looked back out there twenty minutes later, she was squatting again. So, I watched for a few minutes, and it quickly became evident she was having trouble passing something.

Of course, these things always happen on a weekend, or late at night.

Sam, my black Lab, had run a metal wire along her chest cavity on a Saturday afternoon. Meika, my German longhaired pointer, had a stroke after all the vet clinics were closed. If there is an emergency, it seems to be at a time when it is almost impossible to find medical help.

I knew that getting her to the vet on a Sunday afternoon was going to be expensive, but I couldn't let the little dog suffer. So, after a number of telephone calls, my vet agreed to meet us at his clinic, and off we went. A short time and three hundred and fifty dollars later, a one-inch-long willow branch piece was successfully removed from her little poop chute, and all was well.

When she was six months old, it was time to have Sierra spayed. At the time, everyone recommended getting a pup spayed at around six months. Some thinking on that has changed over the years, but that is what I did with Sierra then. If you have no plans for breeding a dog, that is just something for which you plan. The spaying along with vaccination boosters was another hundred bucks.

What I didn't plan for was a torn ligament in the ankle joint of Sierra's right hind leg.

She came up lame during the last part of the hunting season when she was not quite two. A pulled muscle is all I thought it was. My other hunting dogs have come up lame from time to time, and a little rest is all they've ever needed to heal. But when Sierra didn't get better after a couple weeks of no hunting, I decided that a visit to the vet was in order.

Fearing hip dysplasia or some other debilitating long-term disease, I was almost relieved when the vet said that it was a torn ligament and surgery could be done to help repair the damage. If Sierra had been an older dog, with her best hunting years behind her, I might have decided otherwise. But since she was only twenty-two months old, with hopefully a number of good years ahead of her, having the surgery was really the only option. That is in spite of the $850 price tag.

What the vet neglected to tell me when she was giving me all the options for surgery was that there is a twelve-to-sixteen-week recovery time after the surgery. Time when Sierra would have to remain fairly immobile while the repairs healed.

Sierra and my other two hunting dogs were mostly outside dogs. They rarely came into the house, and when they did, they would pant and pace and generally seem uncomfortable. Plus, Sierra never stayed still. She was in constant motion. She was one of those Labs whose whole back end would rotate back and forth when she wagged her tail. And since she was in a continual state of happiness, torn ligament or not, she was always wagging her tail. She also would jump with pleasure when it was dinnertime and whine with happiness when she was around me or other family members. So, confining Sierra for recovery was a real challenge. But we got through it, and the following hunting season, she was back hunting with me again.

That is, until the cranial cruciate ligament in her other leg went.

When I saw her limping after a day of hunting, I had a suspicion that she had torn the ligament in her other leg. I chatted with a veterinarian friend of mine and learned that some dogs are just built with fragile ligaments. Dr. Barb Allard is a longtime friend. We've known each other since I was in high school and she was a veterinary student at Washington State University.

At the time I had aspirations of becoming a vet, so I got a job at Dr. Hank Heffernan's vet clinic in Yakima. I'd work there after school and on weekends, cleaning kennels and examination rooms, and holding dogs, cats, birds, goats, sheep, and every other animal that came into the clinic during examinations. I enjoyed working with the animals, but there were times when I wanted to throttle the people who brought in their pets.

Once, a man brought in a male dog of unknown heritage and asked to have the dog's testicles examined. When Dr. Heffernan did so, he called me in for assistance. The dog's owner had decided that instead of having the pup surgically neutered, he would just put tight rubber bands around the testicles in hopes that they would fall off.

Banding testicles works in sheep, but not in dogs. I won't try to describe the horrible smell that came from the poor pup's testes when Dr. Heffernan went to work on draining the infection from them. It was not pleasant. The bands were removed, the infection drained, and a heavy dose of antibiotics was administered. From there, the dog walked gingerly out of the office to hopefully better days ahead.

"That guy should have rubber bands placed around his testicles," Dr. Heffernan said to me after the man and dog exited the clinic. "See how he likes it."

I wanted to laugh, but I was afraid any quick expulsion of air from my lungs might make me lose the puke that I was barely holding down.

Another time, a man brought an English pointer in because it had been hit by shotgun fire during a bird hunt. I figured some zealous, inexperienced hunter had accidentally hit the dog when he or she was shooting at a bird. Nope, the dog's owner had shot the dog on purpose.

It seems the dog was ranging too far out, flushing birds well ahead of the hunters, and the man got so mad he shot the dog. The pellets were lodged just under the dog's skin, so it wasn't a life-or-death situation, but if I had been a little bigger, a little older, and a lot stronger, I might have had words for the man who brought in the dog. I couldn't believe someone would shoot their own dog, no matter how mad they got at it.

"I've seen it a number of times," Dr. Heffernan said after he plucked some twenty pieces of lead shot out of the dog. "Afterwards, they get to feeling bad, and they'll bring the dog in to get fixed up."

Being only seventeen years old at the time, I was definitely naive. I had trouble believing there were people out there who treated their animals that way. Both of those men were idiots, and they should have never had any kind of pet. They probably shouldn't have had children either, if they had any.

Working at the clinic was an eye-opener and a learning experience. Just from those two experiences I knew I could never mistreat an animal. And I would always make sure my dogs were trained to at least obey the basic commands.

It wasn't that English pointer's fault that it was out there a hundred yards flushing birds. If the man knew anything about the dog he owned, he should have known that most dogs of that breed are hard-running, wide-ranging, and need a great deal of work and training. My guess is the guy was lazy and did nothing with his dog until he took it hunting that day. He got pissed at the dog, an instinctive animal that was finally out of a kennel or off a chain, doing what every molecule in its blood was telling it to do.

The other thing I learned in my two years at the clinic was that I was not going to be a veterinarian. Not that I wouldn't have liked the work, because I would have. Frankly, I just wasn't smart enough. All those chemistry and anatomy classes would have done me in.

I still ended up at Washington State University and lived right next to the veterinary school, but communication and English were more my speed. In what was a surprise to some, including my advisor in the school of communication, I graduated in exactly four years, with a pretty high grade point average.

Luckily, Barb Allard, who was much, much smarter than me, stuck with veterinary school and got all her degrees. Years later, after I told her about Sierra's situation, she made me an amazing offer.

"If you can get her down here, I'll do the surgery at no charge," she wrote in an email from her clinic in Pasadena, California.

While money was always a concern in our household, what with two growing boys who had sights set on college themselves, the offer for the free surgery still wasn't the driving factor in agreeing to Barb's offer.

At the time, there was a relatively new procedure to repair the ligament damage that involved breaking the dog's leg and then doing some other fancy stuff (I told you I wasn't very good at veterinary medicine) that would make the leg even stronger than the surgery that had been done on Sierra's other leg. The vets in our area were still doing the old surgery to repair the back-leg ligaments on dogs, but Barb had done several of the new surgeries and knew exactly what she was doing.

Wanting the best for Sierra, and with the hopes of getting a few more years of hunting with her, Terri and I loaded Sierra into the back of our GMC Yukon. Off we went, headed south, to the home of the Rose Parade and the grandaddy of them all, the Rose Bowl.

Barb was incredibly accommodating, letting us stay with her at her beautiful ranch house. She and her capable crew did the surgery and let us take Sierra home that very afternoon, so long as we promised to take it very easy with her.

We loaded Sierra in the back of our vehicle with a bunch of blankets and several bottles of pills and headed for home. The drive became a white-knuckle affair as a major snowstorm had blown into Northern California. The mountain passes were requiring chains on all vehicles. Or that's what the freeway sign said. I found out later, after spending a bunch of money at a K-Mart (yes, that is possible) for chains, that I didn't need them because four- and all-wheel-drive vehicles were exempt. Still, we took it easy. When some idiot in an all-wheel-drive Audi tried to pass us and started spinning circles before crashing into a Jersey barrier, I slowed down even more.

"Hope those guys have a change of underwear with them," Terri said as she held on tighter to the "Oh God" handle near her door.

We made it home safely, and after several more weeks of keeping Sierra from running and jumping, her leg healed. Life went on, and the next fall she was out hunting with two repaired back legs that would never give her another problem.

I had always wanted one of those expensive hunting dogs, and I got one. It just wasn't how I expected it would be. When someone brings a puppy into their family, they expect there are going to be expenses. Food and health checks and vaccinations are necessities. The other stuff, well, no one plans on that. Sierra was definitely costly. Little did I know that her vet bills would be nothing compared to another yellow Lab that would join our family a few years later.

Chapter 9

"Dogs do speak, but only to those who know how to listen."

–Orhan Pamuk

Fortunately for me, I have had some adventurous bird hunting buddies, and over the years we've hunted several times in North Dakota and even more in Eastern Montana. On each of those trips we've enjoyed some fantastic hunting and great dog work.

It was on our second trip to Mott, North Dakota that Sierra went along as my dog for the hunt. On a previous hunt I had taken Meika, the German longhaired pointer. While she had done well and had maybe the best hunting of her life there, she was getting on in years, and I didn't think she could run hard for three days of chasing pheasants.

Enter Sierra. This would have been only her second year of hunting, before her first ACL problems. She had the desire, and we had found a few birds in her first year around Central Washington, but she was definitely doing more running than hunting.

Part of the issue was when I hunted in Washington, I took every healthy dog I had. My philosophy was the more noses out there working the heavy cover, the better the chances of finding a rooster or two.

It was sometimes hard to keep track of three dogs, and anyone watching from afar might equate our little hunting party to that of a three-ring circus—one without a ringleader. Dogs would be going everywhere, and the hunters would be trying to keep up.

It was definitely organized chaos, but it worked. I think the birds were as confused as everyone else. They didn't know which way to go, so they would often just flush.

There is something to be said for having less chaos too. Less distraction from having a pack of dogs scrambling around is helpful for a young dog, allowing it to hit a hot scent, track it, and flush the bird for the hunter to shoot. So, knowing Sierra would have a better chance at learning what it was all about, I decided to leave the older dogs at home and just take her.

The four days we hunted in North Dakota was like getting her high school, bachelor's, and master's degrees all in one. Mother Nature and Sierra's breeding had given her all the tools. Being in and around great habitat filled with pheasants allowed it to all come together.

On the first morning of our hunt, my friend Merle Shuyler and I—along with his dog Amber, a full sister to Sierra—started out along a dry creek bed with waist-high grass on both sides. In an instant the dogs were on birds, Amber going one way and Sierra going the other. Sierra zigged and zagged, her nose tight to the ground, tail whirling eighty miles an hour. I ran along, just waiting for the inevitable flush, while Merle followed his dog off in the other direction.

In Central Washington, nine times out of ten, the bird that flushes will be a hen. In North Dakota, the odds for a rooster are much better.

When the bird Sierra was tracking—a big, colorful rooster—took to the air, cackling all the way, I had to take just a split second to calm myself. She had done her job, and now I had to do mine. I led the bird, pulled the trigger, and it folded dead in the tall grass. A second later a white dog came out of the grass with the rooster in her mouth. There may be no happier time in a hunting dog's life than when they have a bird in their mouth. As they bring it to their person, they're so proud they could burst. That was Sierra.

In that moment, I knew she had it. She had put two and two together, and now she had the answer. Follow the scent, flush the bird, and if I did my job, she would have a bird to retrieve. Retrieving was her favorite of all. From that moment on she was the best little hunter a person could ever ask for. She hunted close. She hunted hard. And she found birds.

We got eight more roosters on that trip, Sierra and I. The first successful trip of many.

Dogs can't talk, but they sure can communicate. Some of my dogs have tried harder than others to tell me what it is they want. Sierra was one of the best at it.

As is the case with most dogs, Sierra had an internal clock that was set on Greenwich Mean Time. You could set your watch to her daily routine. Most of her communication with me had to do with getting fed. If I was even a minute behind schedule for feeding, Sierra would remind me what time it was. She would start her dinnertime communication by sitting in the backyard and holding her empty dish in her mouth while she stared in the back window. If that didn't work, she would start to bark. If that didn't work, she would go lie down and pout.

Feeding time aside, Sierra would often speak with her eyes. She would look at me, right in my eyes, and try to tell me what she wanted via some kind of telepathic communication. Often it would work.

The time it was most evident happened during a hunting trip to Montana.

I had been drawn for a deer tag, and that fall I was supposed to go with friends to hunt in Central Montana for a week. But a medical emergency in my friends' family threw the schedule into a tailspin. They had to postpone their hunt. Since I had scheduled the hunt as part of my vacation days, I was stuck going when we had originally planned.

Going by myself was an option, but my son Kyle was off work at the same time, so I talked him into going to Montana with me. The plan was to hunt deer for a few days, and then we'd hunt birds for the rest of the week.

Planning a combo trip was a bit tricky because if we were going to hunt birds after hunting deer, having a dog along was almost imperative. The trouble was that the dog couldn't deer hunt with us. Between the fourteen-hour drive to Eastern Montana and the crate time during our deer hunt, it was not going to be much fun for the dog.

Sierra was my only dog with any experience at the time, so Kyle and I loaded her into the crate in the back of the truck, and off we went. We stopped and let Sierra out often, but every time we lifted her (she couldn't jump because of the issues with her back legs) she would do everything but get back in the crate. It only got worse as the trip went along. She would look me right in the eyes and plead to remain out of her crate. I always made sure there was a pad and some fresh straw in the crate. It was plenty big and comfortable, but the longer Sierra was in her crate, the more she obviously hated it.

It took longer than expected for me to shoot a buck. When I did, Kyle and I got it broken down into a big cooler and soon hit the highway north to find some birds.

After a two-hour drive, we checked into a motel, changed clothes, and headed to some open lands near the Missouri River. Finally, Sierra would get to hunt. She did great. Kyle and I got our limits of pheasants with Sierra hunting like a champ.

By this point in my hunting career, I always found motels where the dogs could sleep with me in the room when we were out of town. That night, Sierra ate and quickly crashed on the carpeted floor of our room. Kyle and I showered and got ready for dinner. When we left, I called Sierra to come, but she just lay there and stared at me. I knew exactly what she was saying. "Please don't make me get into that crate again. I'll be perfectly good here sleeping until you get back."

I couldn't say no.

She barely lifted her head when we returned a couple hours later. She wagged her tail a couple of times, then fell back to sleep.

The next morning before we headed out for another hunt, we stopped at a hardware store, and I bought Sierra a doggy bed. We moved stuff from the back seat to the canopy-covered truck bed, then put the doggy bed on the seat. From that moment on, Sierra rode like a queen in the back, close to her people, loving every second of the next two days, including the long drive home.

I'm not positive that she'd had enough of riding backwards, inside the crate, in the back of the truck over washboard, dusty roads. But I do know she was much happier with the new seating arrangements.

The next fall, Sierra and I were to join a few friends and their dogs for a week-long bird hunt in Eastern Montana again. I was working my butt off at the office, putting in long hours for a longtime client. So even more than usual, I was ready for the first bird hunt of the season.

As I prepared to leave the following day, I came home for lunch and noticed Sierra's face was swollen.

Doesn't it always seem to go that way?

I called the vet and luckily, I could get her in for a quick checkup. The doctor took a look at Sierra and thought she might have been stung by a bee on her face or in her mouth. He prescribed an antihistamine and said to keep an eye on her.

"Um, I was supposed to take her to Montana to hunt birds tomorrow," I said to the vet. "You think she can still go?"

"It's your decision, but I would recommend you wait a day or two to hunt, just in case," he advised.

So, I made the trip without Sierra. Being without her made me feel naked the whole time. As it turned out, the next day at home she was fine and could have hunted, but you just never know. Better to be safe than sorry.

That would have been Sierra's last road trip. The next year, she had slowed substantially, and with a new pup coming up that had the vigor to do some serious hunting, I left Sierra at home. She never hunted more than an hour from home after that, and within a couple of years, Sierra was fully retired.

When I loaded the young Lab into the crate for our next long journey, Sierra sat to the side and watched. When I looked into her eyes, I could see her telling me that she was fine with staying home. She knew what a road trip meant. Bumping and jostling for hours on end. No thank you.

When the time came, once again, to send another unbelievably sweet friend off on her final journey, she talked to me then too, using those big brown eyes. When I lifted her onto the table at the vet's office, she looked me straight in the eyes and told me it was okay. It was the right decision. I knew it. And Sierra knew it. She was ready. She told me so.

They say dogs can't talk. Maybe not, but I believe with all my heart they sure can communicate, and Sierra was one of the best at it.

Chapter 10

"The better I get to know men, the more I find myself loving dogs."

–Charles de Gaulle

While I have ended up with a couple decent hunting dogs thanks to impulse buys, I prefer to plan out my puppy purchases.

Before you buy a dog, there are several factors to consider. First, is the question of need. And that question usually came from my better half.

"Do we really need another dog?" Terri asked in a way that told me she would really prefer some time without two or three dogs running our life.

What she didn't know was that as part of my master puppy-purchasing plan, I built in time to *talk* about buying a puppy long before I really wanted to get another one. I was priming the pump, so to speak. Every time Terri would ask the "need" question, I would tell her, "No, we don't really *need* a puppy." Then I wouldn't bring it up for a while. Later, when I really did feel like I "needed" a puppy, it was a smaller hill to climb.

The main factor in the "need another dog plan" is fitting a new puppy into the hunting rotation. About the time an older dog is slowing down and heading toward retirement, a young dog needs to be up and coming. With Sierra slowing down, it was time to start looking for a new pup.

My new puppy plan had a few glitches, however.

First, the puppy parents of my little future hunter didn't do something right. A couple of hunting buddies, Dan McKimmy and Mike Schell, were owners of our proposed puppy pairing. They got their dogs together, but for some unknown reason, their mating didn't take. Unfortunately, nobody knew that for a while.

Dan's dog Annie showed all the signs of being pregnant, but on the anticipated birthday, the babies were a no show. A check by the veterinarian showed that Annie had had a false pregnancy.

Those of us who had wanted a pup from this union of good hunting Labs were disappointed. I may have been the most disappointed, though, because the groundwork had been laid, and the "need another dog" plan was working to perfection on the home front. Even Terri was looking forward to a new puppy.

What to do now? The window of opportunity in my plan was still open, but it was closing fast.

I searched my limited memory bank to see who I knew that might be having a litter of hunting Labs soon. I remembered that my cousin in Nevada had raised some litters of Lab puppies over the past few years, but what were the chances he would have some pups now, and if so, would he have any still for sale?

"You're in luck," my cousin Bill Henry said when I inquired about a puppy. His good-looking yellow Lab had just had a litter of pups. He had three female puppies that were as of yet unspoken for, and one was mine if I could figure out how to get it.

"How would you like to go to Reno next month?" I asked Terri in late June of 2008.

"Sure," was her reply. "What casino are we going to?"

She wasn't too upset when she found out that our twenty-two-hour puppy pick-up marathon wouldn't include slot machines and blackjack tables. We did see a huge portion of Eastern Oregon, some of Northern Nevada and even a sliver of Idaho on our jaunt. Oh, and we spent close to three hundred and fifty bucks on gas! The high gas prices and a 1,600-mile road trip were not part of my original puppy plan.

But in the end, we ended up with a precocious little yellow Lab puppy. We named her Tessa, after the daughter of the Seattle Mariners' great designated hitter Edgar Martinez. This was about the time Martinez was retiring from baseball, and during a special ceremony in Seattle, they introduced his whole family, including his cute daughter Tessa.

"That's a great name," I told Terri when I heard it. We were well beyond having any more children, so I decided to use the name for our next puppy. It was a perfect name for what turned out to be a not-so-perfect dog.

When I picked Tessa up as a seven-week-old puppy from my cousin Bill, he told me that she would have a thick tail like a beaver. A strong, thick tail on a dog that might make long retrieves in the water is a good thing. While I planned to do more upland bird hunting than waterfowl hunting with Tessa, I was still pleased to hear this.

My cousin failed, however, to inform me that our new dog might exhibit a few other beaver-like traits—such as chewing wood and gnawing branches off trees.

I discovered these other habits when I came home from work one evening and discovered a giant hole in my cedar fence.

"What happened there?" I asked, more to myself than anyone who might be within hearing distance.

"Tessa," was the one-word answer I received from Terri.

I nodded as if I understood, but the whole time I stared at the gaping hole in the fence, I tried to imagine how one dog could have created such a chasm.

When I stepped out the back door for a closer inspection of the destruction, Tessa ran up to me, then to the void in the fence, and back to me, tail wagging, as if to say, "See what I did? Isn't it great—did I do good or what?"

"When did the dog learn karate?" I hollered back into the house.

I mean, how else could a dog destroy the cedar planks so completely? There were shards and splinters and wood pieces spread in a ten-foot half-circle. One of those little clown cars could have driven right through the hole, all without the clowns having to duck.

I guess I should have seen the problem coming. A couple weeks prior, I had looked out into the backyard and seen only the two older dogs lying in the warming mid-afternoon sun.

"Hmmmm, where's Tessa?" I wondered to myself.

As I scanned the fence line, I noticed a long yellow bump in the grass right next to the fence—a bump that normally wasn't there. In an instant, the yellow bump was gone.

Out the back door I went, straight to a new hole in the fence that framed a hole dug underneath it. On the other side, peeking through the crack with a big smile, sat Tessa.

"How in the world?" I said to the panting, grinning dog.

Tessa was still a puppy, but a full grown one. She was way too big to go through this opening, or so I thought. It looked like an anorexic Shih Tzu couldn't have wriggled free, but somehow Tessa had, and it was her beaver tail exiting the backyard that I had noticed only moments before.

"Well, come on, get back in here," I said to the happy yellow dog.

And in she came—nose first, paws second. With plenty of squeezing and inching and squirming, she was birthed back into the yard.

I pounded a new fence plank in place over the little hole and figured she would never do that again.

Wrong.

Well, actually I was right. She learned, I guess, that a small hole created too much work. It forced her to become the Houdini of the dog world. A bigger hole made escaping so much easier. And a bigger hole she made. A Seattle Seahawk lineman could have pedaled a tricycle through that hole.

This doggy escape-artist act was new to me. All my other dogs, young and old, had been mostly content to stay in the fenced backyard. In an effort to stop the wood chewing, I placed hog wire over the places where Tessa had gnawed holes, and it seemed to work.

They say that puppies will chew and dig until they are two years old. Luckily for the fence, Tessa moved on to other forms of destruction.

Before Tessa arrived as a seven-week-old bouncing bundle of yellow energy, Terri had some beautiful flowerpots around the back patio. One planter was home to a giant, fruit-bearing cherry tomato plant.

Within a couple of weeks, Tessa totally destroyed the plants in the planters and the planters too. When she had completed her assault on the flora, a person might have thought a bomb had gone off in the backyard. The planters that still had some actual plant growth in them were made up of nothing but stems and sticks. I didn't know dogs liked tomatoes, but I guess Tessa did. Our tomato yield dropped to nothing once she developed a taste for them.

Tessa wasn't much of a digger, but boy did she enjoy tearing stuff up. Dog toys were chewed to smithereens, and if they weren't challenging enough, soon she turned to her dog beds.

One day in early December, I came home to a backyard that was covered in white. It looked like a scene from a Christmas card. The problem was, it wasn't snow, but the stuffing from not one or two but three dog beds. In the middle of the fluffy white stuff sat Tessa, with a big grin and satisfied look on her face.

Naively, I thought once she got the dog bed destruction out of her system, she'd be okay to have a new one.

Wrong again.

At the time, we had two older dogs that enjoyed lying on their dog beds, so I hated to deprive them of that pleasure. It didn't bother Tessa though. I bought three more beds, and Tessa immediately went to work on them too.

I have never been accused of being very smart, and as I look back on it, continuing to buy dog beds, only to have Tessa destroy them, was pretty dumb. In my defense, since the dogs were mostly outside dogs—living in the backyard during the day when everyone was away at work or school—I wanted them to have a nice bed on which to lie.

Tessa had other ideas.

At some point, I either stopped buying beds for the dogs, or she finally grew tired of destroying them, because in her later years, Tessa loved sleeping on her bed.

After the issues with the fence chewing and the bed destruction, I started thinking about writing a book just about Tessa. I had the perfect title: *The Trouble with Tessa*. She was only a year old, and every day she was doing something unusual, maddening, or funny.

Take for instance the time Tessa decided to open one of the Christmas packages under the tree. It was cold and snowy that winter right before Christmas. As we were apt to do, we left the dogs in the house when we went to a family event. At night, the dogs came in and slept on any surviving dog beds in the laundry room. To deter them from leaving the laundry room in the middle of the night, we put one of those kiddy gates in the doorframe.

For some reason, our dogs always respected the little gate, even though they easily could have jumped it or pushed it over. But it just never happened. Or it didn't until that night in December when Tessa was about six months old.

Evidently, her nose and her Lab appetite had enticed her enough to knock down the doggy gate and check out the Christmas packages. In one of the nicely wrapped boxes, amongst other things, was a bag of fun-sized Snickers.

From the mess that greeted us when we walked through the front door, it was clear that one of the dogs had ripped into the box and then chewed open the bag of candy bars. There was no question who the culprit was.

There, sitting on the couch surrounded in brightly colored Christmas paper and candy bar wrappers, was Tessa.

As I looked at the mess, she wagged her tail and looked at me like, "Look what I did. Nice, huh?"

"How many candy bars were in that package?" I asked Terri, like she should know.

"I don't know, maybe twenty-five or thirty," she answered. Then she asked, "Isn't chocolate supposed to kill a dog?"

I was too busy counting candy wrappers to notice the hint of hope in her voice.

"I only count about a dozen wrappers," I said. "That means she ate the rest. If the chocolate doesn't get her, all that aluminum foil might."

Every time one of us would speak, Tessa would smile and look at that person while wagging her tail.

"I don't know," Terri said. "Our dogs have always eaten a little chocolate here and there, and it's never hurt them. Let's just watch her and see how she does before we do anything rash."

And that's what we did. Tessa adjourned to a slightly torn bed in the laundry room, fell asleep, and never showed any ill effects from her Snickers feast.

I had forgotten about the little episode until one afternoon a few days later. I was looking out at the backyard, and the snow, which had fallen a week earlier, was now sparkling in the sunshine. As I walked out to examine the glittering ground, I saw that in the dog droppings scattered around the yard were tiny pieces of the silvery packaging from the miniature candy bars.

Another story for *The Trouble with Tessa*.

Chapter 11

"Before you get a dog, you can't quite imagine what living with one might be like; afterward, you can't imagine living any other way."

–Caroline Knapp

I thought Sierra was going to be my "expensive" dog. Little did I know that Tessa would blow Sierra's record all to pieces.

Tessa was about a year old when I noticed her lower eyelids drooping. They made her look a little like a basset hound. I thought I had seen most dog maladies by now, but this was a new one for me. I foolishly hoped the droopy eyelids would correct themselves, but after a month or two I took Tessa to the vet.

"Ectropion," the vet said almost immediately after looking at Tessa's eyes. "We can fix that with a little surgery."

Of course, it had to be done. In some of the places we hunt, our dog's eyes collect plenty of weed seeds and other matter even with normal eyelids. But with these big drooping scoops under her eyes, Tessa would have been miserable.

The surgery seemed straightforward, and it wasn't terribly expensive. The issue with surgery around the eyes, or anywhere really, is dogs like to mess with the wounds as they are healing. I knew that, but when the vet tech told me they would need to put one of those lampshade cones around her head to keep her from licking the incisions, I had to think about it for a second. How was she going to lick the sutures and incisions right below her eyes? I didn't say anything. I figured the main reason the vet ordered the torturous device was so Tessa wouldn't scratch at the incisions with a paw.

If you've ever had a dog who needed to wear one of those devices, technically called an Elizabethan collar, it is kind of funny, and kind of sad. I call it the cone of shame.

Tessa hated it.

From the day she was burdened with the cone collar until the day she finally had it removed for good, she was constantly running into things. People too. If you weren't watching, Tessa would run the edge of the cone right into your leg. Young children were the most susceptible, as she would take their legs out from under them in an instant.

When Grandma visited, Tessa and her lampshade were banished to the outdoors.

Thankfully, the cone of shame only had to be worn for two or three weeks, and soon she was as good as new. Unfortunately, her good health would not last long.

As was the case with all my other dogs, Tessa loved to hunt. And like me—probably because of me—she loved to hunt pheasants. Labrador retrievers were originally bred to be waterfowl dogs, but over the generations they turned into very competent upland hunting dogs too. That's the great thing about the breed—Labs will hunt pretty much anything that flies.

Tessa would hunt grouse or partridge or quail, and she would even retrieve ducks, but she lived to hunt pheasants. She made many trips with me and my friends to Eastern Montana to hunt the plentiful pheasants there, and we would hunt most Saturdays during the bird season in Central Washington. I never could tell just how good her nose was, but when Tessa hit the field, she was off and hunting.

As was the case with all my other dogs over the years, Tessa liked to know where I was. That being the case, she wouldn't ever hunt too far out. She'd constantly check in with me and then take off again to find more birds.

What she hated most on our hunts was standing still. *Hated* it. So much so that if we ever paused for more than a minute, she would start whining this loud, annoying whine while staring up at me. The second we started walking again, she'd stop whining and take off.

Because of that, and because I never acquired a taste for duck, we never went duck hunting. For Tessa, sitting quietly in a blind would have been like being waterboarded along with several other tortures. If I ever got invited to join a friend for a duck hunt where we would set up decoys and sit in a blind, I would either decline the invite or go solo, without Tessa.

"Bring your dog," the friend would say. "She'll love it."

"You don't know her," I would respond, thinking about the annoying whining. "I'll do us all a favor and leave her home."

Over the years, I don't know how many pheasants she retrieved. A lot. One of her very first retrieves sticks out in my mind. Most of the others I have forgotten, but this one was special.

We were hunting birds in the lower Yakima Valley and somehow we got separated from the group of guys and dogs we were hunting with. In an effort to catch back up to them, we cut through an apple orchard.

I wasn't really even thinking about hunting at that point. I just wanted to get through the rows of apple trees and back to the big weedy field where everyone else was hunting.

So, with head down, walking quickly, I wasn't paying any attention to Tessa. When I looked up, though, she was on point. My first dog Zeb would point, but my other Labs were strictly flushers, so it caught me off guard to see her frozen, pointing at the base of a small apple tree.

The brain is an amazing thing. So many thoughts can go through your mind in a millisecond.

At first, I didn't believe what I saw. The grass next to the trunk of the apple tree couldn't hide a sparrow. Was she actually pointing? Probably a quail, if anything. It couldn't be a pheasant though. Not enough cover.

"C'mon," I said to Tessa.

That was all she needed. She moved quickly at the trunk of the tree, and out flushed a big rooster pheasant. Evidently, it had been hiding in a hole in the ground.

The bird flew so close to me I could have reached out and touched it. Shaken, stupefied, but not totally paralyzed, I turned, and as the bird flew down a small brushy ditch that dropped into a little ravine, I pulled up and shot.

The rooster disappeared over the rise in the hill, and then everything was silent. I looked around for Tessa, but she was nowhere to be found.

I thought I might have hit the bird, but I wasn't positive, so I walked over to where I last saw it. The draw was full of brush and grass. I had no idea where or even if the bird had fallen, so Tessa would have to come look. Where did she go, I wondered?

Standing at the spot, I listened to hear where she might be. Again, silence. So, I whistled for her.

All of my dogs learn quickly that when I whistle, they are to come. Not a big whistle. Not a metal or plastic whistle like a referee. Just a soft little purse-your-lips whistle.

Pheasants are not stupid birds. The second you step into a field and start blowing a whistle, you might as well be screaming at your dog because the birds hear you and take off. Quiet is the key. So, a quiet whistle is what I use.

But when I stood above some brambles and whistled for Tessa, I got no response. Then, way, way down at the bottom of the ravine

I saw her pop out of the brush and start running back to me. In her mouth was a very alive rooster pheasant.

My shot had only winged the bird, and Tessa had tracked it down and made the long retrieve back. I hate bad shots, but long retrieves are the best. And that was a good one.

Over the next few years, Tessa pointed occasionally, and when she did, I knew to be ready, because something was going to be there.

It was not far from that long retrieve where Tessa got into a very scary situation.

Several friends and I were hunting a Feel Free to Hunt field on the Yakama Reservation, as we did most Saturdays in the fall. Tessa was a strong hunter and had a never-give-up attitude, something I loved about her. But this time, it about got her killed.

This Feel Free to Hunt field sat across the road from private property. The owner of the property disliked hunters, and many times, when someone was hunting the Feel Free to Hunt field, he would patrol up and down the road to make sure no one crossed onto his land.

It wasn't until this hunt that I learned the guy had gone from patrolling his property to turning two pit bulls loose when he saw hunters nearby.

As long as the dogs stayed on his property, there'd be no issues.

Once again, it was my shooting—or more correctly, poor shooting—that got us into trouble.

Tessa flushed a rooster that, instead of flying deeper into the Feel Free to Hunt field, flew back at the property being patrolled by the pit bulls. I shot, and the bird went down, but it was only winged. Of course, it ran straight at the road and the private property. Actually, I didn't know which way the wounded bird had run until I saw Tessa tear off in that direction, hot on the bird's scent.

The next minute or two are a blur in my memory. I remember seeing the two pit bulls running through the Feel Free to Hunt field, and they were on the same line as Tessa. Again, I'm not very smart, so I thought those two dogs were tracking the bird too. As I looked at them, Tessa crossed the fence next to the road, then crossed the road and headed onto the private property, following the scent trail of the running bird.

A second later, the two pit bulls went across on the same line, and in an instant, they were attacking Tessa. I couldn't see the attack, but I could hear it. It was sickening.

At the time I was fifty years old and still in decent shape, but my legs felt like they were stuck in concrete as I tried to jump the barbed-wire fence and get to the dogs.

When I finally got there, probably twenty seconds later, the dogs were tearing into Tessa, one at the front, the other at her rear. She was doing her best to fight them off, but she was overmatched.

As soon as the dogs saw me, they stopped the attack and started backing off. My shotgun was ready. If they had advanced at her again, or at me, I was ready to shoot. Luckily, they turned and ran.

Tessa and I got off the private property as quickly as we could, and when I knew we were safe, I took a good look at her. The dogs had ripped a couple of pretty good holes in her hind legs, so off we went for an emergency visit to the vet clinic.

After cleaning the wounds, a couple dozen stitches, and an antibiotic injection, the vet sent us on our way. Tessa was hunting again within a couple of weeks. We never went back to that field, and even today I avoid it, although those dogs are probably long dead.

The night after the attack, I had nightmares of those dogs ripping into Tessa. If I hadn't gotten there as quickly as I did, I am positive they would have killed her. To this day I still get sick to my stomach when I replay the events of that morning.

A couple of years after the pit bull attack, I noticed Tessa was having trouble walking after hunting for even a half day. Once she lay down, she had trouble getting up and could hardly walk. She was only six years old, so the issue wasn't old age.

Another visit to the vet was in order, this time during regular office hours. I thought she must be suffering from the early stages of hip dysplasia. Then again, my cousin said he had done a great deal of research on Tessa's mother's and father's pedigree. Neither had dysplasia in their background.

The vet didn't immediately rule out dysplasia, but he noticed that Tessa's ankle joints were not right. They were larger than normal, and after a couple x-rays, the vet determined she had some serious arthritis in those joints. When I asked the vet if there might be a correlation between the pit bull attack and the arthritis, he said it was possible.

Over the next couple of years, we went through several types of treatment on Tessa's legs, including the first ever stem cell transplant in our area. The procedure was fairly new in the animal world, and medical experts had seen some incredible reversals by putting the stem cells into the arthritic areas. My vet clinic was looking for a dog to try the new procedure on. They said if I paid for the stem cell harvest at a laboratory in California, they wouldn't charge for their labor.

Even with their generous offer, the procedure was going to cost me several thousand dollars. If Tessa had been even a couple years older, I probably would have passed. But with her still being in the prime of her life, I felt like it was worth it to try to keep her legs as healthy as possible. I read all the literature from the stem cell operation in California. After looking at the success they'd had, I decided it was worth the effort and the money.

In the meantime, the vet had set up several laser treatments for Tessa. They would bring her in, and with a special tool they lasered the two back leg joints in an effort to make it less painful and easier for the joint to move.

Each procedure required everyone to wear goggles, including Tessa. Surprisingly, Tessa took the goggles in stride. She sat through the treatment looking like the pilot of a biplane.

According to the brochure, the cold laser therapy is a noninvasive procedure that uses light to stimulate cells and increase blood circulation. At the correct laser wavelength, pain signals are reduced and nerve sensitivity decreases. The procedure also releases endorphins which act as natural painkillers.

I didn't see much difference after the treatments, but Tessa didn't seem to get any worse either, so it was definitely worth the try.

The stem cell treatment was more invasive. The first part required Tessa to have surgery under anesthesia. The vet made an incision on her side and removed significant amounts of fat. The fat was then shipped overnight to the laboratory in California where they harvested the stem cells and express shipped them back to the vet. The stem cells were then injected into the ankle joints where they hopefully would start reversing the arthritis.

I had cautiously hoped this radical new treatment would work, but the short answer is, unfortunately, it did not.

My vet injected Tessa's stem cells into the joints twice. But to no avail. Again, maybe it helped curtail the advancement of her arthritis, but it didn't shrink the size of the joints or eliminate any inflammation.

Tessa never seemed to improve. She could hunt for a few hours, but the next day, walking was a real challenge. I hated putting her through it, but she wanted to go hunting so badly. Often, I would take her along and try not to work her too hard.

There were a couple changes in our lives that helped keep her going for a while longer. First, my next Lab joined the pack when Tessa was seven. She loved playing with the pup, and it definitely made her younger, or at least it seemed like she felt younger. Her legs didn't work very well, but she sure tried.

My vet once told me that dogs (especially Labs) have an incredible threshold for pain. I could tell. As she got older, every step was painful for Tessa, but she pushed through it without so much as a whimper.

Dog-feeding time became a challenge at the Phillips household as we tried to help Tessa be more comfortable. We fed her a special food, different from what the other dogs ate, and we were always trying to get a plethora of pills into the mix.

Tessa would take a half of a tiny little pill for chronic arthritis in her back legs. And she also took two doggy-strength glucosamine/chondroitin pills. To help all the medicine go down, I would plop a half-can of dog food on her kibble, hiding the pills in the sloppy stew.

It worked pretty well, in part because Tessa liked to eat and was not terribly discerning.

Then after hearing a radio commercial from one of the local health food stores about their availability of CBD oil for dogs, I decided to check it out.

According to the internet—and you know, if it's on the internet, it has to be true—there are some advantages to giving dogs CBD oil. All of it is anecdotal, of course, but there seems to be enough positive results reported by dog owners out there who have tried it with their pets.

One website said that, while there's no conclusive scientific data about CBD benefitting dogs, some dog owners have reported that the treatment has reduced their dog's pain, especially neuropathic pain, as well as reduced seizures for their pet. And CBD can be used as an anti-inflammatory. Some people also use it with their dogs for its cardiac benefits, anti-nausea effects, appetite stimulation, anti-anxiety impact, and for possible anti-cancer benefits, although these benefits are all anecdotal.

Tessa was going on twelve years old at the time and had been hobbled with arthritis for years. So, when I read some of the information about it, I thought it couldn't hurt. I bought a small bottle of CBD oil and began giving it to her on a biscuit morning and night.

Now, I'm not going to say the drops cured poor Tessa of her arthritis, but I'll be darned if it didn't perk her up. She started running more, and better. It was noticeable almost overnight. The CBD oil was the only new addition to her diet and medications.

After telling a hunting buddy about what we saw with Tessa and the CBD oil, he started using it with his ten-year-old Lab. She would be extremely sore after a few hours of hunting. But after my buddy started giving her the CBD, she began bouncing right back without any noticeable soreness. Unfortunately, the effectiveness of the oil seemed to wane after a few months of use. I guess I could have tried giving her progressively higher doses, but that didn't seem like a sustainable solution.

The other thing that kept Tessa going was we moved out into the country.

For thirty-three years, we lived in the city. Our little three-bedroom brick rambler was a nice house in a nice neighborhood with a big yard. We raised our two sons in that house, and it was home to every one of our dogs, from Zeb to Sierra.

It was also my grandma's house. We purchased it from her in 1982. I remember going to that house for about every holiday from the time I was very young. Sunday dinners, Christmas Eve, Easter and all kinds of other celebrations were held in that house. Those gatherings included my grandma and step-grandpa, my great aunts and uncles, my mom and dad, plus several of my mom's siblings, and all kinds of cousins.

Add all the other life events a family celebrates in between holidays, and you'll have a sense of how many great memories this house held.

Terri and I were raised in the country, and while I was happy in the brick house, I always yearned to have more elbow room. No longer did I want to hear the next-door neighbor screaming at their kids, or another neighbor's dog barking endlessly at nothing.

Our chance to move to a beautiful new-to-us home came in 2015. The house sits on a little over four acres and includes a small orchard of three varieties of cherry trees. I grew up picking cherries on my paternal grandfather's orchard in Naches, so having some cherry trees to care for, and a bigger place, was a good fit for us. Terri was also raised on a small cherry ranch, so the new place just felt like home.

No one enjoyed the move more than Tessa though. Even with back legs that didn't work well, she went exploring, looking for whatever she could find. She and our younger Lab would try to corral ground squirrels and rock chucks. Because the younger Lab was hell on wheels, sometimes Tessa would be in just the right place when a squirrel doubled back. She only caught two that I remember, but when she retrieved the little varmint to me, you would have thought she was two years old again.

It was all so much fun for her, and I was so glad she could spend her last few years wandering the orchard and sleeping in the cool orchard grass.

When Tessa started falling, then having issues with controlling her bowels and bladder, I knew it was time. Once again, I had to make the call to pull the plug. I've hated it every time, and frankly, it has only gotten more difficult. I just kept telling myself that it was the right thing to do, and that extending her life would have been more for us than for her.

It wasn't the best timing in retrospect, but I took Tessa into the vet three days before Christmas. Her pain was over quickly, and after a good cry, I left her remains to be cremated. When I got home, the house felt a whole lot emptier. Because it was.

There's a saying I've seen from time to time: "No longer by my side, but always in my heart."

That is true with all my dogs, but especially with Tessa.

Chapter 12

"The bond with a true dog is as lasting as the ties of this earth will ever be."

–Konrad Lorenz

Over the years I have hunted with, or been around, a number of different dogs. Almost all have been sporting dogs. Some were of questionable heritage, while others had pedigrees as long as Mohamed Shehata's world-record wingspan.

Almost every dog breed in the world has some kind of working background. Back in the day, they were either herding dogs or hunting dogs. Some were big enough to take on a lion. Others were fast enough to catch rabbits and gazelles. Others were long and short, to go into holes after whatever lived there. Some would withstand incredibly cold temperatures to retrieve birds in cold waters, over and over again. You get the point.

Oh yeah. And some of them point. Most of the pointers will point if they smell anything gamey, including porcupines, skunks, cats, and what-have-you.

Still, you will sometimes see a breed of dog do something that it maybe wasn't bred to do.

Take the pair of Saint Bernards we spotted one winter day in Moxee.

My buddy Rob Robillard and I were on one of our typical Saturday pheasant hunting trips, driving to one of our favorite hunting spots when I looked out the car window and spotted a man walking beside a big irrigation drain with the two large dogs.

Now, the Saint Bernard is a breed of very large working dogs from the Western Alps in Italy and Switzerland. The dogs were originally bred for rescue work by the hospice of the Great Saint Bernard Pass on the Italian-Swiss border. Movies and TV shows have cast the Saint Bernards as rescue dogs at avalanche scenes, and each will have a cask of whiskey or some other liquid tied around their neck.

The two dogs Rob and I spotted that day, way back in the late 1970s, were nowhere near Switzerland, and neither were toting casks on their collars. The man with the shotgun was obviously hunting along the drain, but the dogs weren't out searching for anything—they were just walking along with the man.

"Pull over," I said to Rob. "I'd like to see what's up with those dogs."

We did pull over, and when I asked the man what the dogs were doing with him, he was almost surprised at the question.

"They retrieve my ducks," he said.

"Really?" I asked.

"They're quite good retrievers," he said. "They love hunting with me."

In the almost fifty years since, I have not seen one other Saint Bernard out hunting, let alone two. I still kick myself for not getting a photo of the man and his big brown-and-white dogs. But believe me, it's true. Or at least it is true that we saw the dogs with the man. I, unfortunately, didn't get to see them retrieve a duck.

While I have only owned Labs, and one sometimes cranky German longhaired pointer, over time I have hunted behind many other types of bird dogs. I have hunted with Chesapeake Bay retrievers, golden retrievers, German shorthaired pointers, Weimaraners, Vizslas, Brittany spaniels, springer spaniels, cocker spaniels, wirehaired pointing griffons, and several other breeds of more questionable heritage.

Some have been good, and others have been not so good. Some you envy so much you wish to someday own a dog like it. Others you hope will run off and never come back.

The ones you would just as soon not come back are the ones that, predictably, take off like a cheetah as soon as they exit the rig. Screaming or whistling won't slow them for a second, and the next time you see them, they are just a silhouette on the skyline a half-mile away, flushing birds here and there as they go.

One time, I was hunting ducks with some friends down in a huge wildlife area in Central Washington. It is mostly known as a duck-hunting area, but that day we were hunting valley quail in brush so thick that you'd literally have to crawl through some of it.

It was an area where having a good hunting dog was an absolute necessity. We were a couple miles from the truck, in the middle of nowhere, and as we walked and crawled through the brush, we came nose-to-nose with a poodle. At least it looked like a poodle.

"Is that a poodle?" I asked the guys I was hunting with. They all thought it was.

"Some poor lady in Mabton must be heartsick that her dog has run off," one of them said.

Then there was a whistle, and the dog turned and headed toward the sound.

When we finally popped out of the brush, there were three hunters, including an acquaintance of mine, Ralph Thompson, walking through the grass. The dog was working back and forth in front of them, just like it knew what it was doing.

I said hello to Ralph, then asked the obvious question.

"Say, is that a poodle you're hunting with?"

"No," Ralph said with a laugh. "It's an Airedale."

Now Ralph is a respected judge in our area, and I had no

reason to believe he might have been ribbing me. I had heard of Airedales before but had never seen one in real life, so I had to take him at his word.

Later, Ralph told me that the dog was owned by a friend from Seattle. And he said it was really a pretty decent hunter, except that it hunted very slowly. A slow hunting dog can be good at times, unless you want to hunt more than a couple fields in a day.

I wondered how it did with the horribly incessant cockleburs in the area. The dog didn't have flowing, feathery hair like my German longhaired pointer did, which was a burr magnet. But the curly, longish hair of that Airedale had to pick up the burrs too. If it really was an Airedale, and not a poodle like we originally thought.

Then there are the dogs that go above and beyond the call of duty. I remember the story that was told to me by Dennis Evans of Toppenish one day. It seems he had a Chesapeake Bay retriever named Zoey that made a pretty nice retrieve during a duck hunt.

Evans was hunting one of his favorite duck spots in the lower Yakima Valley when he shot a duck. It promptly fell into the pond about fifty yards from land. Zoey, ten years old at the time, swam out into the lake, picked up the bird, and retrieved it to her admiring master.

No big deal, right? Most retrievers can make that kind of a retrieve with one paw tied to their tail.

Wait, did I forget to tell you that Zoey went and fetched that duck while towing a boat?

As is the case with many dogs that just love to retrieve, Zoey suffers from premature blind evacuation syndrome. For you non-hunters, that means the dog will run out to retrieve a bird before it has actually been shot. Ducks will almost never try to land in a bunch of plastic duck replicas with a dog splashing about. The ducks fly away before the hunters can shoot them, which, in turn, makes the hunters very, very upset.

So, dogs that have trouble staying in the blind need to be restrained. That way, the ducks will fly within shotgun range, which is the whole reason for sitting out in the freezing cold at the crack of dawn.

Hunters with early leaver dogs have come up with a variety of ways to keep their four-legged partners in the blind. Some hunters who have tied their overly exuberant dogs to their belt, or another article of clothing or body part, quickly learn that is not a good idea. They have learned this because the dog has jerked them off their feet, out of the blind and, in some rare cases, into the frigid water.

In an effort to control Zoey's enthusiasm, Evans resorted to tying the dog to his eight-foot pram.

He uses the little camouflaged boat to get to where he wants to hunt, and to help place decoys. When he is not using the boat for transportation, he places it up on the bank next to his blind and turns it into a dog hitching post. Even though the boat is not overly heavy, it takes some pretty good muscle to move it into the water.

As the story goes, Evans shot a duck and went to release Zoey for the retrieve, but she was already on her way to the bird.

"She turned the boat around, towed it off the bank, all the way out to the duck, and then back to me," Evans said.

Chesapeake Bay retrievers are usually big, strong dogs, having been developed to perform under the toughest conditions. So, it really isn't a big surprise that Zoey would overcome a little thing like being tethered to a small boat in order to fulfill her retrieving duties.

Cold water. Even colder air temperatures. Tied to a boat. Old and achy. I think I would have told my human hunting partner to "go get it yourself." But not Zoey. She did it all happily.

And that, in a nutshell, is why you just have to love dogs.

My friend Dan McKimmy thought he was getting a German shorthaired pointer when he picked a little brown puppy as his next upland hunting dog. Dan thought the puppy with longer hair and unusual markings looked a little different from the rest of the litter.

"It looks like a springer," Dan said to the man selling the puppies.

The man seemed a bit offended at that suggestion and told Dan there was no way another male got in with his female shorthaired. But as the puppy grew, it became evident that something in the breeding process had gone awry. The little puppy, which should have had long legs and very short hair, was just the opposite, with shorter legs and longer, spaniel-type hair.

Dan named the dog Jack, and of course, whether it was a full-blooded German shorthaired or not, he wasn't going to trade him in. As it turned out, Jack became a pretty good hunter.

The first time I met Jack, I asked Dan if the dog was a springer spaniel. Dan's answer was, "No, he's supposed to be a shorthaired pointer, but he must have some springer in him."

Besides Jack's obvious spaniel appearance, he also hunted like a springer . . . with a little bit of beagle thrown in. The pointer part of the breeding was nowhere to be found.

On our typical pheasant hunts, a group of us will spread out with our dogs and head into a big weedy field or asparagus patch. With some of the dogs, you might not see them again until the end of the field. But you always knew where Jack was, or at least you would when he got on a bird, because he would start barking. It wasn't baying like a beagle on a rabbit. It sounded more like a bloodhound on a bear.

Jack was a true flusher, so when you heard him barking, you had better get up there, because a bird would be taking flight soon.

I always enjoyed listening to Jack's happy bark when he was on a bird, especially if he was getting closer to me. I knew that if Jack was heading my way, barking as he came, there was a good chance I was going to get a shot. As soon as he flushed a pheasant, Jack would stop barking and go off to find another.

Jack did have a couple of unhealthy habits. The first was his proclivity for chasing cars. He also had a taste for frogs. Or he thought he did.

One day, Dan and Jack were walking up the sidewalk to their house when a little green frog hopped out in front of them. Before Dan could say "No," Jack grabbed the frog and swallowed it. A minute later, he was having convulsions and foaming at the mouth. Dan didn't know what to do.

Jack came out of the convulsions, and pretty soon he was back to normal—or what normal was for Jack. Dan called the vet and asked if eating a frog would hurt him. The vet told him there were no poisonous frogs in the area so not to worry about it.

Evidently, Jack was cured from eating more frogs because as far as Dan knows he never came close to another. The car chasing did him in, though, as Jack was hit by a speeding UPS truck. It was a shame because Jack was a hoot to hunt with. When he was barking after a bird, you could tell he was loving every second of it.

Speaking of beagles, I hunted with a guy one time who used his rabbit dog for pheasants. That little beagle was a blue-collar rabbit hunter in a fancy pheasant-hunting world.

When the guy unleashed the little brown, black, and white dog, it disappeared into the brush. Judging by how fast it took off, I thought it might never come back. Finally, as we walked along, we heard the baying of the beagle at the far end of the field. I looked way, way down there, and pheasants were going everywhere. Well, everywhere except toward us.

Now, if you have never hunted rabbits with beagles, here is what they do. The dogs run and run and run until they catch the scent of a cottontail, and then they follow it until they find the furry little critter. At that point, if a rabbit could fly, it most likely would. But since bunnies can't fly, they run. Quite often they run in circles.

When a beagle hits the rabbit scent, it starts baying. Eventually, the dog pushes the rabbit toward the hunters. Then bang, hasenpfeffer.

Rabbit hunting with beagles is actually quite fun. Mostly because as you watch and listen to the dogs, you know they are doing what they were put on this earth to do.

But back to the pheasant-hunting beagle. You have to give the little guy credit because he'd run until he about dropped from exhaustion. The thing was, the pheasants were very poor rabbit substitutes. Every time the dog got close enough to the birds to try and turn them back toward us, the pheasants would fly. Almost always out of shotgun range.

I'm sure there were times when some pheasants would double back. In fact, that is a favorite trick of veteran roosters. So, occasionally the guy with the beagle may have had a good shot. But that day, there were none, and it was quite frustrating for the hunters and the other dogs.

It was hard to blame the beagle. He was hunting the way generations of beagles have hunted before him. It was how they had been trained to hunt. It was what his genetics told him to do.

My hat's off to the guy for getting his beagle out. It was just a square peg in a round hole situation. He needed to take the dog down by the river and let him chase rabbits to his heart's content. And maybe he did. But I got the impression they hunted pheasants primarily. I'm guessing they didn't eat many fried pheasant dinners on Sunday afternoons.

Chapter 13

"If your dog doesn't like someone, you probably shouldn't either."

–Jack Canfield

I would be remiss if I didn't tell you about a dog we had only briefly. Her name was Dakota, and she was a black Lab. Like Cassie, Dakota was purchased sight unseen and she wasn't papered—the person selling the Lab pups just wanted them to go to good homes. The seller knew I was a hunter, so she sold Dakota to me for a hundred dollars.

Back then—with two growing boys eating us out of house and home, plus a mortgage, a car payment, and ambitions of saving for college—spending a bunch of money on a dog was just not in the cards. Dakota seemed like a good deal to me.

And she was—for my mother-in-law.

Here's what happened.

Dakota was an adventurous little pup. In the late spring, after I brought her home from Portland, we would leave her in the backyard with Cassie and Meika, our two older dogs. But Dakota would get tired of being stuck with two dogs that just lay around, so she'd sneak through a tiny gap in the fence and go visit the neighbors. After seeing where she got out, I would put up more fencing, but she'd just find another crack in the fence and take off.

We lived in a nice neighborhood, but still there were plenty of cars driving by. She just couldn't be out where she might get hit. So, I built her a wire kennel about four feet high. It didn't have a roof, but I wasn't worried. A jackrabbit couldn't have jumped out of that thing.

One late afternoon, while the dogs were out in the backyard, our doorbell rang. At the door was a neighbor with Dakota in her arms.

"Is this your pup?" the girl asked.

"Yes, it is," I said, taking Dakota from her. "Thank you so much."

The pup and I went to the backyard where I inspected the little kennel. It was still standing right where I'd left it. I looked around the edges in the grass. No holes had been dug. How had she escaped?

I put her back in the kennel, and then went into the house and watched her for a while from a window where she couldn't see me.

She stayed in the kennel for about five minutes, then, like a monkey, she started climbing the sides of the kennel. I couldn't believe it. When she made it to the top, she kind of flopped over, hit the ground, and took off for the big fence. There, she found her escape hole, and out she went.

I was there to meet her when she came around the corner. She was so happy to see me, I couldn't scold her. A wire top went on the kennel that day and from then on, Dakota stayed pretty much corralled.

When the training started, I worked with Dakota just as I did all my other hunting dogs before her. I'd bang pans around her at dinner time and pound nails into wood . . . all the things you do to get a dog used to loud noises. Plus, with the boys and their friends always around playing in the backyard, Dakota dealt with the constant commotion like a champ.

Come September, I took her out and shot a .22 rifle around her, and with the other dogs all excited, Dakota took it in stride. Next up was a shotgun.

One early September afternoon, I took her to one of my favorite grouse-hunting spots. Here, she could get used to being around live birds. If I remember right, I shot two grouse that afternoon, and because she was still a pup, she didn't quite know what was going on. But when I got her to the downed birds, she acted like all my other dogs. She was quite excited and enthralled by the new smells, and by having a bird in her mouth. All was going well.

After a while, I looked up and saw an archery hunter walking up the road right on the ridge. I thought, what the heck, I might just go over and say hi and see if he'd seen any grouse.

As Dakota and I walked his way, he sort of waved us off. I stopped, but it was too late for Dakota. She ran right up to the guy and jumped up on him. And, to add injury to insult, she hit the poor guy right in the groin.

He doubled over with a grunt, and in an instant, Dakota was trying to lick his face. I rushed over to grab her, and as I pulled her off, I looked over and saw a nice three-point buck walking up the hill about twenty yards away.

"There's a buck," I whispered to the guy.

He tried to get it back together enough to get an arrow nocked, but after watching the commotion for a few seconds, the deer bounced off over the hill.

"Geez, I'm sorry," I said.

"My buddies were driving that draw to push the deer to me," the guy groaned. He was not happy.

I grabbed Dakota and hustled back over the ridge to our truck as quickly as I could. All I could do was apologize.

Some time after that first hunting season something happened, and Dakota became gun shy. When I took her out the next year, any time a gun was fired in the field, she'd turn and run to the truck. Later, after she connected the sight of the guns to the noise she hated, she'd start shaking as soon as the shotgun came out. She was a sweet dog, and I hated to see her in such distress.

Not long after that, my mother-in-law Mavis lost her dog. One day, when we were discussing Dakota's gun-shyness, she offered to take her.

I know there are ways to get a dog over the fear of gunshots and loud noises, but having a fifty-hour-a-week job, plus coaching basketball and all the other things that go on in a family's life, I just didn't have the time or energy to make it work.

Dakota loved it at Mavis's house, and whenever we visited, she would be so happy to see me. She had a good, long life, and besides the Fourth of July and maybe New Year's when folks set off booming fireworks, Dakota was quite happy.

The other black Lab that briefly lived at our house was our son Kyle's pup, Cali. She was definitely a special "grand-dog" and a perfect companion for Kyle.

A typical Labrador, Cali was a chowhound. She would eat anything at any time. Kyle even bought her a special dish with posts in it so that Cali had to work for each kernel of kibble. Otherwise, she ate her food too fast.

Kyle lived in some cold places in Idaho and Montana, so in the winter, he would keep Cali inside his house. She quickly learned how to get into the wastebasket under the kitchen sink, and more than once Kyle came home to find garbage strewn around the place.

One time Kyle left a pound of butter on the counter. Somehow, Cali got up there and ate every stick, wrappers and all.

Another time he left Cali with a co-worker for a couple of days while he was away on a business trip. In that time, Cali ate the majority of a ten-pound bag of dried cat food. Cat food is not good for a dog, but Cali seemed to have no aftereffects.

When she was young and Kyle was living near a pear orchard, Cali would occasionally escape the backyard and go see what she could find among the fruit trees. She ate a bunch of green pears and came home so bloated that Kyle thought she was going to burst. But again, she didn't suffer any damage from that.

Another time, she snuck into the orchard and found a worker's unguarded ice chest. Kyle said she brought home a can of Budweiser, punctured it, and drank it. He wasn't sure if she'd already enjoyed the worker's sandwich or burrito before having a brew to quench her thirst.

Cali gobbled up more than one quail too. Most of the time, she dutifully retrieved the little birds, but sometimes hunger must have overcome her, because she'd swallow the things whole if she had a hankering.

I knew she was going to be a chowhound right from the get-go. Kyle was having us watch the eight-week-old black ball of fur while he was away for a couple of days. After I took Cali and my older dogs outside to pee, I gave them all a small dog treat. My big dogs would chew them. Cali, despite being so small, swallowed the dog-bone-shaped treat like a horse pill.

I panicked.

How could such a little dog swallow a treat that barely fit in her mouth? I just knew she was going to choke to death. Here I was, in charge of his brand-new pup. How was I going to tell Kyle she choked on a treat I gave her?

She didn't choke, though, and it was the first of many times when Cali's ability to scarf something whole amazed me.

As crazy an eater as Cali was, she was a great hunter. She pointed if the birds held, and was an excellent tracker and retriever. Although she never brought back a downed bird that was still alive. If the bird was dead when she found it, no problem. She'd pick it up and bring it to Kyle. But if the bird was alive, Cali would give it a good chomp to kill it before she retrieved it.

I'd guess that when she was young and went to pick up a wounded rooster, the bird spurred her. Not wanting that to happen again, she would make sure each downed bird was good and dead before she brought it back to Kyle. It was an aggravating little habit, but having a hard-mouthed dog that retrieved anything from anywhere was better than having one that dropped birds at the first sign of a struggle.

Cali was also a jumper. She could easily have been a dock dog. From the minute Kyle brought her home, she was jumping off the three-foot porch never even touching a step. She'd jump at the back window at feeding time, and as an adult dog, she could jump high enough to look through the kitchen window above the sink.

Despite her athleticism, stairs either confounded her or scared her. This was especially true of the stairs at a motel we stayed at on a bird hunt in Montana. The flight up to the rooms had open air between the steps, such that you could see through them to the landing below. Cali would not walk up them. Kyle had to carry her.

Even regular stairs bothered her, and she oftentimes had to be coaxed to go up them. Coming down, she would just take two steps and jump.

Kyle was a single guy, so having a dog for company, and as a hunting companion, was well worth some of the messes Cali created. She was a sweet, loyal dog, and it was a very sad day for all of us when the vet told Kyle that Cali had a brain tumor and had to be euthanized.

We'll all remember the jumping, wiggling Lab, the one that was always happy to see everyone, and even happier if they had a treat in their hands.

In her later years, shortly after my dad passed, my mom decided she needed a dog in her life to keep her company. I didn't quite know how it was going to go, but at first blush it seemed like a good idea. She was all alone in a spacious house, and I thought having a dog might help bring some life and sunshine back into her home.

Mom decided she wanted a Havanese. One of her friends had two dogs of that breed, and my mom liked the size of the dog and its temperament. I'd never heard of them before, but Havanese have long, silky hair, don't bark much if at all, and don't shed. They were originally bred as a companion dog to the Cuban aristocracy in the 1800s, and apparently they've earned the nickname "Velcro dog" because they stick so closely to their owner's side.

Mom named the little dog Molly, and she definitely fit the Velcro nickname. Wherever Mom went, Molly went. She turned into a really nice dog and was good company for my mom.

It didn't take Mom long to settle into her old ways with dogs in the house, however. Molly liked to eat, and my mom hated to say no. So, the little dog became pudgy. Mom fed her treats constantly, and because she said Molly wouldn't eat her dry kibble, she started fixing her meat for dinner. I can't tell you how many times I left our dinner table after having a hamburger or some kind of casserole, only to find Molly eating filet mignon at Mom's house.

When I asked Mom why she was feeding the dog expensive meat, she just said, "Because she likes it."

"Of course, she does," I said. "What dog wouldn't?"

"She won't eat her kibble," Mom explained.

"If you would stop feeding her treats and prime rib, she'll eat the kibble when she gets hungry enough."

Molly was with my mom right up until the minute Mom died. It was sort of surreal. Molly and Mom were together, and then, when Mom died, Molly left and wouldn't return to the bedroom. She knew somehow her favorite person in the world was gone.

Knowing that she would most likely go before Molly, Mom had made arrangements for one of the Havanese-owning friends to take Molly.

We called the friend shortly after Mom passed, and the friend said she would come right away. In the meantime, though, one of the neighbor ladies stopped by to check on Mom, and hearing that she had passed, offered to take Molly. When the neighbor said that, I looked at Molly, and she ran over and got behind my leg. The little dog had a look of fear. Her eyes were saying, "No, no, not with her."

It was as plain as day. I had no idea what her history was with the neighbor lady, but I do know that even if she was supposed to go with her, I wouldn't have let it happen. I would have taken her first.

Luckily, a bit later, the friend arrived to retrieve Molly. We let Molly out the front door, and she ran to the friend's open car door. That little dog jumped inside like she knew this was the plan all along, and they drove off together, to the next chapter in both their lives.

Frankly, it was a bit eerie what happened that afternoon with Molly. I think I had known for a long time that dogs have some incredible intuition about people and the things happening around them. But the day my mom died really hammered it home.

Chapter 14

"My little dog—a heartbeat at my feet."
                                        –Edith Wharton

As I write this, the latest in our line of dogs, a black Lab named Bailey, is sleeping on the bed behind me. She has been a constant companion since I retired and my book-writing career started. She loves being with me and, I have to confess, the feeling is mutual. I wouldn't say she is the perfect dog, but she comes as close as any dog has.

After health issues in some of my previous dogs, I was hoping to find a dog that would be athletic and healthy. I wanted a female, and I wanted to get her while Tessa was still able to do some hunting. Tessa's bad back legs were hindering her hunting stamina, but I thought if I could get my next pup while Tessa was still somewhat mobile, then it would be good for both dogs.

Fortuitously, the search for our next pup led me to a breeder not ten miles from home. Rattlin' Ridge Labs, operated by Joan St. Hilaire, has been putting out excellent Labs for three decades. They have done all the research and testing on their dogs for health clearances. The dogs that are part of their breeding program are guaranteed to be free of hip, eye, or other genetic health problems.

I reached out to Joan, learned a little more about her dogs, and soon found out there was a litter of pups coming in September. The dogs had pointing in their background, and while she wouldn't guarantee any of the pups would point, there was a strong likelihood.

I sent her my down payment and waited to hear about the litter.

A look at Rattlin' Ridge's website and Joan's Facebook page will reveal many great-looking dogs. Most have ribbons attached to them or placed around them. I didn't care how my dog would work in a test. I wanted her to hunt and to be a good family dog.

When the litter's eleven pups were five weeks old, Butch Schlagel and I went out to see them. Butch was also looking for a pup, and when I told him about Rattlin' Ridge, he too sent in a deposit.

You never know what you're going to get with puppies. But if you do your homework and choose a pup from a litter of well-bred dogs, the chances of getting a good one certainly improve.

I wanted a female—I knew that for sure—so that eliminated six of the eleven puppies. Still, five of the cutest little black puppies were left to choose from. There was some due diligence to be done first, including hovering over them, picking them up and loving on them, and watching as they chased blowing leaves, chewed on sticks, attacked one another, and frolicked around. I know—a real tough assignment.

I wasn't going to take one home yet. Because the puppies were still too young to leave their mother, I would have to wait three weeks to make my final decision. But man, I didn't know how I was going to pick just one.

Joan had the pups in colored collars. From the time they were born until the time they went to their new forever home, the pups were in the same color of collar. When Butch and I first looked at the pups, I had my eye on the green-collared one, plus a smaller one with no collar.

Both were still available when we returned three weeks later, but I still was having trouble deciding. Luckily, Terri was along for the picking process, so I turned it over to her. Women's intuition and all. Plus, I had always been the puppy picker. It was time for her to pick our next dog.

Frankly, I would have been happy with either puppy, but I thought she had made an excellent choice when she chose the one with the green collar. The seven years since have proved Terri right. Bailey has been a fantastic dog. She's bright, athletic, hunts hard, is almost perfect in the house, and is a joy to have around.

There were times during those first few months, however, when I didn't know if Bailey and I were going to make it. Actually, Bailey was never my concern. As a young pup, she was happy as a lark, living the life of leisure and participating in other quickly learned habits, both good and bad.

Because Bailey was born in September, she didn't come home with us until November. By then there was snow on the ground, which effectively turned her into an inside dog. It was a new experience for us as we usually had our dogs spend lots of time outside.

Luckily, Bailey was a smart pup. She was potty-trained quickly, and by directing her to the proper chew toys, we avoided major furniture mishaps. I have heard of puppies chewing up doors, baseboards, sheetrock, and furniture legs. The way we averted that was by having Bailey in her crate at night, and for naps during the colder days. It worked just fine.

She was the first dog we ever crate-trained. Without it, I am not sure what we would have done. Bailey learned to love her crate in short order. It was large enough for her to stretch out and move around in, but kept her confined when she needed to be. There were times when she went to be in the crate, just because it was "her" place.

By springtime, Bailey was close to her adult size, so she could spend the daytime hours outdoors. She still slept in her crate in the laundry room at night, next to her big sister Tessa.

Speaking of Tessa, she helped with Bailey too.

When Bailey first arrived, Tessa would lie down and play with her, nearly putting Bailey's whole head in her mouth as they wrestled around. She was always gentle, even when Bailey was practically swinging from Tessa's ears. Once in a while during their growling playtime, I would hear Tessa yelp. I knew full well that Bailey had hit a sensitive area with her needle-sharp milk teeth.

Playtime with the retrieving dummy turned into a game of cat and mouse. First, it was Tessa getting to the dummy well before Bailey and basically dragging the puppy back to me at the end of the toy.

The tables turned quickly as Bailey got bigger and faster. Tessa, with the bad arthritis in her back legs, soon couldn't keep up with Bailey. So, Bailey had to learn to sit and stay; that way, Tessa could have her turn at retrieving. It was a good lesson for the puppy.

What Bailey loved most, though, and still does, was the one-on-one retrieving training we did. This work revolved around a dummy with pheasant wings attached to it. It was the most fun part of her day, which often included digging holes along both side fences, chewing on sticks, running back and forth along the back fence while the little dogs in the adjoining yard yipped and barked, and pestering Tessa when she was fast asleep.

Bailey also loved our outings. We would jump in the truck and run out into the country, then walk through some of my favorite hunting spots. Both dogs enjoyed it, and even early on, before Bailey had an idea about what she was looking for, she followed Tessa and sniffed out every corner of the field.

As the years have gone by, both Terri and I have softened on our dog rules. Our first Lab Zeb spent almost all his time outdoors, unless it was just too cold for him to be out. Our other dogs over the years were pretty much outdoor dogs too. They would sleep in the house at night during the winter, but other than that, they lived in the backyard.

I provided solid houses with lots of insulation and clean bedding for them, so they lived a good dog's life. But their time in the house was limited.

Bailey's arrival changed that. When she was just nine weeks old, she figured out how to jump onto the couch. We thought it was so cute, we never stopped her. Today, she will ball up on the couch or in a chair, and you hardly know she is there.

Of course, Bailey being on the furniture is all my fault. But I didn't see anyone else in the house scolding her. That train is now *way* far down the track. It will never be turned around.

And while Bailey doesn't sleep on our bed when we sleep in it, she has developed the cute habit of wandering into our bedroom when no one is paying any attention and napping on our bed.

Yep, that's my fault too. But again, I don't hear Terri scolding her when she sees Bailey all stretched out on the bed.

There's an old adage that says you should not, under any circumstances, spoil your hunting dog. Hunting is their purpose in life, and turning them into a house dog will make them soft.

Bailey is seven now, and it hasn't been a problem. She still hunts hard. She is smart. She has pointed dozens if not hundreds of quail and pheasants and has made some really nice retrieves. What more could you ask?

If she wants to stretch out on the couch after a hard day of hunting, I'm okay with that. In fact, I am usually right there beside her. Yes, there is plenty of black dog hair on the couch and on one of her favorite chairs, but a little vacuuming usually takes care of that issue.

I never thought I would see the day when Terri and one of our dogs would share our furniture, but it happens frequently now. It is a very endearing sight.

Practically from Day One, I knew Bailey was going to be a hunter. Hunting was bred into her, and it is what she lives for the most. Early on, I hoped she would be a pointer. Fortunately, she confirmed that trait not long after we moved to our small orchard when she was six months old.

From the day we arrived at the new place, Bailey would take multiple daily romps through the trees. Our new closest neighbors are quail, gray diggers (ground squirrels), rock chucks, gophers, mice, an assortment of different lizards, as well as robins and other birds. When she was young, those things would all get equal amounts of Bailey's attention.

While she always enjoys getting a snoot full of quail, one of Bailey's infatuations has always been gopher mounds. She will dig and dig and dig. If a Yugo were to drive down one of our rows of trees, I swear it would disappear into a gopher hole widened by Bailey's efforts. When I holler at her to stop digging, Bailey will just peek out of the hole, her face covered in dirt and a big smile. Once in a blue moon, she'll even catch one of the little pests and happily retrieve it to me.

The occasional success on the gopher front has made her even more determined to catch a gray digger. She has come close a couple times, but they don't play fair. The squirrels have this annoying habit of running under one of the coniferous trees in the orchard, and while Bailey is going in behind them on one side, they will exit on the other. Bailey looks and looks, but to her it is like they have magically disappeared.

The pesky squirrels will practically destroy a garden, and they will climb the cherry trees and eat the cherries, which infuriates me to no end. So, I wouldn't mind if Bailey caught one now and again. Bailey is fast, but the ground squirrels are faster. Once they hit the safety of their burrows, they will chatter right in her face, which makes her even more determined the next time she happens to spot one out in the open.

The varmints that really have her perplexed are the rock chucks. They will find refuge under a giant rock, then whistle and whistle at Bailey as she circles them, trying to figure out how she might get under that five-hundred-pound rock. She is still confounded by it all.

I'm not as sure about the lizards. Bailey discovered the little reptiles early on around our place. During the summer, they seem to hang out anywhere there are rocks or block retaining walls. I knew Bailey was going to be a pointer because from the time she was six months old, she's been pointing the little reptiles.

On our morning walks, Bailey will hit all the known wildlife hot spots on our mini-circuit of the acreage. She will hit all the rocks and bushes where she has seen the quick little lizards, all the while keeping her eyes open for wayward squirrels. She'll hit a line of brush where the quail like to loaf and will then go into the orchard to begin excavating a fresh gopher mound. It is all so much fun.

Watching her desire to hunt all the wild things around our new place, I knew Bailey would be a hunter.

Every dog is unique, and Bailey is different from any of the other Labs that have shared some of my life. Unlike a lot of Labs, Bailey is long and lean. And she's as fast as a greyhound. When you watch her run, it almost looks like she's flying, eating up ground effortlessly as her body uncoils and stretches.

And the joy she exudes while running is infectious. If a dog could smile, you would see it in Bailey's face as she glides over the terrain, sailing over sagebrush and logs. Running is flat-out fun for Bailey.

She also takes playing fetch to another level. All my other Labs were good retrievers, and playing fetch was fun for them. But none have sprinted with as much enthusiasm as Bailey. Sprint to the dummy and sprint back. Over and over and over again. She never seems to tire of the game. I think if my arm held out, she would do it all day long.

Bailey's first hunting season was what I would call a success. When she had just turned one year old, I took her to Montana to hunt pheasants. She hit the fields in Eastern Montana in early October having never hunted anything in her young life besides squirrels and robins. But by the time we headed back to Washington a few days later, she was hunting like a seasoned dog.

As is the case with most young dogs, Bailey sometimes hunted too far out. There were times, too, on an open field without much cover, she'd hit all four corners of the field before the rest of us had walked a hundred yards. But she was learning.

She found birds, sometimes even pointing them if they would hold. At first, she would chase after the hens or the roosters that didn't get shot, but in about a day of hunting, she learned there was no use in chasing the flying birds. Bailey found out it was the ones falling from the sky she needed to find.

The rest of that hunting season proved to be good training too, and we both learned a great deal. I learned how to handle a dog with endless amounts of energy, and Bailey learned not just to hunt, but to hunt as a team. There are times when Bailey gets so excited that she forgets her old hunting partner is not Usain Bolt. Even in my best days, I don't know if I could have kept up with her. So, we kept working on her hunting closer to me, and having her come to a slight whistle. Now, at age seven, she has that mostly figured out.

All my past Labs have been wonderful dogs. They have all been good hunters and companions, but Bailey is really special. She's a smart dog and aims to please. It took a while, but now I think she has the hang of it. Oh sure, there will still be a few hiccups going forward, but there have been fewer and fewer of those as she has matured.

Chapter 15

"No matter how little money and how few possessions you own, having a dog makes you rich."
                                                    –Louis Sabin

Did I mention that Bailey is a little different from the other Labs we've had in our life? She is a walking, barking dichotomy.

Bailey is the fastest Lab I have ever had. She can run like the wind when she wants to. But she is also the slowest walking dog I have ever had. When it is time to come in from playing or from our walks, her head drops and she slinks along at the speed of a sloth. She reminds me of a three-year-old kid who is told it is time to come take a bath. You can almost see her pouting.

Most hunting Labs are flushers, meaning in the field they scent trail a bird and then try to push it into the air. Bailey is a pointer. She has the pointing trait in her genetics, and even though the breeder told us there was a good chance she would point, they made no guarantees.

Not that I wanted or needed a pointing Lab. I've had Labs that would point occasionally, and while it's cool to see them do it, that certainly wasn't going to be the determining factor in buying a new puppy. I was more interested in finding a pup from a litter that had been selected and certified to be free of some aggravating and possibly career-ending hereditary health issues. If she pointed, fine.

Maybe it's the pointing part of her breeding, or maybe it's just the disposition of Labs in general, but Bailey is extremely patient. Or, I should say, she is extremely patient at times. She will sit for hours on the edge of our driveway and stare down into a canyon where rock chucks and gray diggers live.

On the other hand, if she wants something, like a walk, she will sit and stare at me for a minute, then whine and put her head in my lap. If that doesn't work, she will jump into my lap and lick my face.

Unlike most Labs, or at least most of the Labs I've had, Bailey doesn't beg to be petted. If she has her mind on something else, she will actually get perturbed when someone tries to scratch her behind the ears.

My other Labs were constantly nosing my hand or arm, wanting me to give them some attention. Bailey never does that. Although now, as she has gotten a bit older, she will allow us to pet her and rub her shoulders and belly. She obviously likes it, because when we do it, she makes a noise not unlike a pig grunting.

Labs are considered water dogs. Some of my other Labs would go out of their way to jump into any creek, river, pond, or lake we came across, just because they loved the water. Not Bailey. She'd just as soon not, thank you. Not that she won't jump in the water. She will, like when we are working on retrieving or when a bird drops in the pond. Otherwise, she's quite happy on terra firma.

And maybe the most un-Lab quirk of them all is Bailey's apathy toward food. This was a first for us. Every other Lab in our life would eat like they'd not been fed in days. I've seen Bailey walk up to her food dish, sniff some steak pieces, chicken, bacon, hamburger—you name the meat—and literally walk away. What dog does that?

Our veterinarian says she is not food motivated. Man, if I could get that trait transferred over to me, I'd be thirty pounds lighter.

Yes, Bailey eats. But she does so when she is hungry. That might be tonight, tomorrow morning, or who knows when—a few nice pieces of pork tenderloin sitting in the dish be damned.

It didn't take Bailey long to fit into life on a cherry orchard. She would accompany me every time I went to water or spray weeds or mow. And she particularly liked it when I patrolled to keep the starlings and sparrows from devouring the ripening cherries.

Actually, describing it as an orchard might be a bit inaccurate. We have a little over four acres with all kinds of coniferous and deciduous trees. Scattered in amongst the other trees, we have nine cherry trees of different varieties. We call it an orchard, but it might be better described as a grove. Or maybe a stand. How about an *orchardette*?

Whatever you want to call it, the cherry trees usually have a nice crop of fruit, and the birds will descend on the fruit-laden branches in huge numbers about two weeks before the cherries are ripe enough to pick. Not being one to idly stand by and let the birds just eat my fruit, I have declared war on the winged freeloaders. Armed with my little Sears single-shot .22 rifle, loaded with birdshot, I will patrol the "grove" morning, noon, and night.

Dutifully by my side is Bailey.

The first year on the orchard, Bailey really got into hunting the cherry snatchers. She even started climbing the cherry trees, looking for the feathered thieves. It was amazing to watch her climb the trees. You'd have thought she was part cat.

The next year, instead of waiting for me to determine the patrol schedule, Bailey would come to wherever I was at the time and sit down and just stare at me. When I stood up, she would run to where I kept the .22 rifle, as if to remind me where I had put it. Then she would go to the door and prepare for our departure.

If I tarried for more than a minute, she would come to me and start barking in an effort to speed up the process.

When we finally headed out the door, Bailey would sprint to the closest cherry tree and start looking up in the branches. If she spotted a bird in a tree, she would sit down and just stare up at it. If the bird flew out of the tree, she would watch it until it left the orchard. And then she would run to the next tree, where she might even climb it for a closer inspection.

The birds are not stupid, and they would catch on to our little game. Most would flee at the sight of Bailey and me walking out to the trees. But some were a little greedier and more reluctant to leave the smorgasbord. As a result, some would end up dining on their last Rainier or Bing.

That is always Bailey's favorite part of the hunt. She loves to retrieve, and a fat starling gets as much attention as a pheasant, quail, or her retrieving dummy. Hey, anything to help scratch the bird-retrieving itch during the months between hunting seasons, right?

One day, instead of packing the little rifle in and out of the house a half dozen times, I unloaded it and stashed it up in the crook of a cherry tree. I figured doing so might also lull the birds into a false sense of security, seeing me come out to the trees unarmed.

Bailey saw me do this, and when she finally convinced me it was time again to go out on bird patrol, she ran right past her normal stop at the first cherry tree and raced to the rifle in the tree. She looked at the rifle and then back at me as I walked out to the orchard. Then she looked to the rifle and again back to me as if to say, "In case you have forgotten which tree it was in, here is the rifle right here."

Over the years, I have had dogs that would get all excited when I pulled my hunting boots or my shell vest out of the closet. And they definitely knew it was time to go hunting when I got the shotgun out of the gun safe. But Bailey has taken this thing to another level. She's always reminding me of where I've placed hunting gear.

Now I just need to teach her to remember where I put other things such as my car keys and my hunting license.

Another bird, at a different time of the year, gets Bailey going. Usually for a month or so in the early spring, we get visited by a flicker or two. The woodpeckers land on our roof and pound away at the side of our house. It sounds like a mini jackhammer or a little machine gun when they start in.

So now, each spring, we play a game of "get the woodpecker." It consists of lots of barking and running around the house, and there might even be a curse word or two shouted in frustration. I won't say whether it's me or Bailey who is cursing.

Again, it all started a few years ago. I was sitting and reading the paper one morning and heard the familiar hammering of a woodpecker on the side of the house. Now, just know I am a bird lover at heart. I learned at an early age how to identify most of the birds around our area, including their calls, and I love to watch them. But when one comes and starts drilling holes in the freshly painted siding, that's when we're going to have some issues.

When the northern flicker came knocking, I went to the gun safe, grabbed my high-powered air rifle, and headed to the door.

This is where Bailey got involved in the fun little game. As soon as she sees me bring out any kind of gun, for any purpose, she thinks it's time to go hunting. In other words, she gets incredibly excited. She starts yipping an unbelievably loud, high-pitched bark and spins in circles.

Needless to say, all the dog commotion sends the flicker flying post-haste.

Now, when Bailey hears the bird pounding away at the side of the house, her ears go up. She will turn and look at me with an expression that says, "Did you just hear that?" I don't know how she figured it out so quickly, but she knows the stuttering noise means I'll be marching for my air rifle.

So far, the flicker has bested us. Fine with me. Bailey, on the other hand, would like to see that bird fall from the sky; that way, she could retrieve it.

I don't like the idea of shooting the bird, but I will if I have to. We spent several thousand dollars painting our house last summer, and the last thing we need is a hole in the siding where yellow jackets can build nests, let alone a hole big enough for a woodpecker's home.

I have thought about employing some turkey tactics on ol' Woody Woodpecker. I am thinking of dressing head-to-toe in camouflage and sitting in the shrubbery to await the arrival of my long-beaked nemesis. If I stake him out, I am going to have to do it in stealth mode though; Bailey can't be aware of my strategy. There's no way she would sit still with me for that.

Funny enough, Bailey is usually very patient when it comes to hunting. She has learned to sit quietly in the duck blind for long periods of time. And when we take a break during our pheasant hunts, she will sit patiently and wait for her old, overweight hunting partner to catch his breath. Other Labs I've had, including Sierra and Tessa, wouldn't sit still for two minutes. They'd whine and make a fuss, all because they wanted to be out there finding more birds.

But this woodpecker deal is a whole different ball of feathers for Bailey. She's more determined than I am to get the roof rattler. It is so much fun for her. I kind of hate to take the fun away, but I will if I have to. It's the principle of the thing. There are thousands of trees surrounding our little abode. That's enough wood for a lifetime of pecking.

So far, the flicker follies have ended in favor of the hammering bird. It will quickly get tired of Bailey yipping and twirling around the wild-haired human lurking about and fly off. That's fine with me. As long as the pounding ends.

Through the years, my different dogs have had an assortment of maladies and injuries. Bailey is my first dog to have allergies. I didn't even know dog allergies were possible.

I first noticed it after running (her, not me) through the weedy fields around Central Washington. I have always tried to work my dogs into hunting shape before the season, and taking them to run through the fallow fields is a great place to start.

After a few days of this pre-season training, Bailey started scratching and scratching. When the scratching got worse, I figured it was time to go see the vet. Turns out she had a rash in several places on her undercarriage, indicating she was allergic to something.

I had noticed her belly would be red at times when we got home from hunting, but I just figured the rash came from running through a range of prickly, noxious weeds. I thought it would go away.

Nope.

She needed a special and quite expensive shot, plus two weeks' worth of two different antibiotics.

The other thing she started doing during this time was what the vet called reverse sneezing. It is actually a condition called paroxysmal respiration. Dogs rapidly suck air in instead of blowing it out—making it effectively the opposite of a sneeze. It seems very bothersome to the dog, and when Bailey would go into a reverse sneezing fit, she'd come to me for some kind of relief.

I would plug her nose and rub her throat, which were ideas I found on the internet to help, but until she got the allergy shot and medications, the reverse sneezing fits would hit her again and again.

Trying to feed a food-agnostic dog her medication is a real challenge. Hiding the pills in meat has worked on occasion, but sometimes Bailey just decides she is not hungry and won't eat anymore, including a fat chunk of pill-infused hot dog. Other times she somehow chews her way around the pill, leaving it just as nice and new as when it came out of the bottle.

Now, in advance of hunting season, I take Bailey in for a preemptive allergy shot, which seems to help.

Have you ever heard of "cold water tail?" I hadn't either. But let me tell you, it's a thing, and based on Bailey's movements and reactions when it hit her, the symptoms must be very painful.

She came down with the malady after a long, hard day's hunt one year in Montana. She and I had jumped in the rig and driven to Butte to meet up with my son Kyle and his Lab Cali. We planned to do some early-season partridge and sharp-tail grouse hunting.

When Bailey and I left Washington in mid-September, it was a perfectly pleasant seventy-five degrees. After spending the night at Kyle's in Butte, we got up early and drove east for a couple hours, right into the teeth of a cold front. Montana being Montana, a wintry storm hit. Kyle and I had the gear to handle it, but Bailey was still acclimated to summer.

After spending a hard day running in wet, cold grass and brush, she came down with this painful condition that affects the muscles at the base of the tail, causing it to droop unnaturally.

Being the worry-wart doggy daddy I am, I decided she needed medical attention. We found an emergency veterinary hospital in Butte and took Bailey in. An incredibly nice vet there did an examination, including x-rays, and determined Bailey was suffering from "limber tail syndrome" or "dead tail," a syndrome that is relatively common in sporting dogs and is the equivalent of a sprain. Fortunately, the issue will fix itself with a little time and rest. Medications can help with the pain, and non-inflammatory drugs can shorten the duration of the episode.

So, with three bottles of doggy drugs in hand, the vet sent us out the door, assuring me Bailey would be doing better in a few days. She said she just needed a little rest, and then Bailey would be fine.

Two days later, Bailey was back to being herself, wanting me to throw her retrieving dummy and itching to hunt.

The other health issue Bailey developed has been much scarier than reverse sneezing, rashes, and droopy tails.

Bailey is a smaller Lab, weighing around sixty pounds, and she is built for speed and endurance. She stays in the best shape of any dog I have ever owned; after all, she loves to run and never overeats. So, I was taken aback, and actually pretty spooked, when Bailey seized up after hunting hard one day when she was two years old. Luckily, I saw her stop, but after having my Lab Sam get skewered on a wire, I was sure something like that, or worse, had caused the seizure.

When I got to Bailey down in a small draw, she couldn't move. Her tongue was hanging out, and her eyes were rolling. I had no clue what to do.

Fortunately, I was hunting with an emergency room doctor. He grabbed Bailey, walked her over to the tailgate of my truck, and started lightly pouring water on her. Within a few minutes she could raise her head, and by the time I was halfway to the emergency veterinary clinic, she was lying normally in the back seat of the truck. The vet gave her a thorough assessment and found nothing wrong with her. So, I watched her for a couple days, and she seemed fine.

Then during the next hunting season, it happened again. This time I saw it coming.

Bailey had run hard for a few hours, and when she went by me after a friend had shot at a bird, she got wobbly and then seized up. By the time the friend doubled back to the truck with the bird, Bailey could sit up.

Another trip to the vet and another examination showed no real cause for the seizure. Naturally, I went home and took to the internet. I went onto one of the dog pages I follow and, after describing the situation and symptoms, I asked others if anyone had had a similar experience. Boom. I quickly had all kinds of answers.

Some thought it could be a genetic disorder called "Exercise-Induced Collapse." But Bailey's breeder had both the dam and sire cleared of EIC, so the likelihood of that was slim.

Probably, according to the vet and several folks online, Bailey had become hypoglycemic. On those two occasions, she had just run out of the nutrients she needed to keep going.

It seems other hard-hunting dogs have this same issue. The remedy, if you can call it that, is to try to keep their internal fire stoked during the day with carbohydrates and sugar.

Ideas on what to feed dogs as booster treats run the gamut from Nutri-Cal paste to Hostess powdered sugar donuts. Others suggested putting a little Karo syrup in her drinking water during the hunt and adding Dyne, a high-calorie liquid supplement, to her food before the hunt.

I have never been a big fan of feeding a dog their normal meal right before the hunt. Doing so has been known to lead to gastric dilatation, commonly called a flipped stomach, a problem with deadly consequences. But I needed to get her fueled for the hunt somehow, then keep her fueled during the day.

For the next several weeks, the UPS driver wore a path to our door delivering stuff I ordered online to try to help with the issue. Again, we hunt a bunch, and those two episodes were rare, but I didn't want it to happen again if I could help it.

Now when we hunt, I carry two extra bottles of water for Bailey, and I stop and get her to drink as often as she will. Plus, I fill a pocket with stuff to feed her so her sugar levels stay up. She'll eat an Oreo cookie sometimes. And she'll eat a small PayDay bar from time to time. I've tried other doggy energy bars, but my finicky eater will just turn her nose up at those. It is a real challenge, but so far, with a little diligence on my part, she has not had another seizure.

I want to keep it that way. There is nothing worse than seeing your dog in distress.

Chapter 16

*"After years of having a dog, you know him. You know
the meaning of his snuffs and grunts and barks. Every twitch
of the ears is a question or statement, every wag of the tail is
an exclamation."*

–Robert McCammon

For forty-three years, I had the same routine. Monday through Friday I would be up by seven, get ready for work, head out the door by eight, put in my eight or nine hours, then head back home. Weekends were spent doing kids' stuff, yard work, and, when time allowed, some hunting and fishing.

That routine all changed in 2021 when I retired from the everyday grind. Now, I am on a new schedule, one that is not dictated by work duties or kids' activities. Today my schedule is set by a black dog named Bailey.

Here is what my typical day looks like now:

6:30 a.m. – Bailey wakes up, stretches, wanders into the bedroom and stares at me. This means she is ready to go out for her morning potty walk. Sometimes I am up and reading the paper, but other times I'm trying to get a few more minutes of sleep. Nope, not going to happen.

6:45 a.m. – After checking the perimeter of our little orchard, Bailey is ready to play. So, we go grab the retrieving dummy and play fetch. At this time, we work on her commands, including hand signals, which are old hat to her. This is pure fun for her, but it also helps keep her in shape.

7:15 a.m. – Somewhere in the next half hour, after catching her breath, Bailey is ready to go for our morning ride. I'm not quite sure how this routine began, but now we jump in the truck and head for town. There, I get my morning caffeine, and Bailey and I share a chicken strip. If I lollygag around the house before we go for our morning ride, she will come and stare at me until I remember it's time to go.

7:45 a.m. – Home from our jaunt to town, I head upstairs to take care of emails or write. Meanwhile, Bailey takes her first nap of the day.

10:00 a.m. – With the nap over, Bailey comes up to my writing room and sits and stares at me, telling me she needs to go for another walk. Actually, it's a good reminder for me to get up and move too. This is the time when we head to the orchard to mow or fix irrigation risers or whatever else needs to be done.

Noon – We stop for a lunch break. Bailey gets a snack, and within minutes she is into her second nap of the day. This nap will be a good one. If I'm tinkering around the house doing some chores or working on the computer, she'll nap for hours, sometimes until three or four o'clock.

4:00 p.m. – Time for another walk. Bailey will come remind me, and off we go. This will be the shortest of our three walks, with another perimeter check of the orchard.

5:00 p.m. – Dinnertime for dogs. Our old, now-departed Lab Tessa was fanatical about eating at five. Bailey, who couldn't care less about food, got into the five o' clock feeding schedule during the Tessa years. Now, she continues to tell me it is time to be fed, even though most of the time she will let the food sit in her bowl until the spirit moves her.

6:00 p.m. – Post-dinner walk. She may not have eaten, but Bailey is ready for our long walk of the day. We'll walk through the orchards and spend time searching for rock chucks and squirrels. It's the most fun time of day, except for maybe playtime in the morning.

7:00 p.m. – Nap number three. For Bailey, not for me, unfortunately. It's a short nap, but hey, a nap's a nap.

8:00 p.m. – Time for yet another perimeter check. Who knows what creatures have wandered into our yard in the past few hours.

9:00 p.m. – One last quick walk for the last potty before bedtime. If Terri and I get caught up in the Mariners game or some other program, and Bailey is ready for bed, she will once again come and remind us it is time to go out. If we're not quite ready for bed, Bailey will head for hers and crash.

After doing this since June of 2021, Bailey has me obediently trained. I'm not sure what she does during the days I'm off fishing, but I believe she misses the routine.

Frankly, it has been good for me too. No longer needing to be at work each morning, Bailey's walk and playtime get me up and going. In an effort to stay in decent shape, the three or four walks each day is good medicine.

My daily routines used to be set around work and family activities. Today, a very punctual black Labrador retriever sets the schedule. I wouldn't have it any other way.

Bailey communicates differently than any of my other dogs have. She rarely barks, and if she does, it is at a stranger, or when she is excited about something. Most of the time she just grunts, which makes her sound like a little pig.

If there's no dog food in her dish when she finally is hungry, she'll go to it, sit down, and grunt. When she needs to go outside, she'll walk up to me, stare into my soul, and grunt.

One evening, she walked up to me and started grunting without any clear motivation. I knew she couldn't be hungry because she'd just eaten. But as soon as I stood up and headed for the door, she followed me out. Once outside, she went to the bucket of dog water and took a big drink. She then went back to the door. I let her in, and she went about doing whatever it was she had been doing before. It wasn't like she didn't have water in the house. Because she did. But for some reason she wanted outside water, so she came and let me know.

Sometimes during the middle of the night, I will be awakened by the persistent little grunts. Almost always she needs to go out for an emergency piddle or poo.

My wife Terri jokes about how I can hear the almost inaudible Bailey but that when our two boys were screaming babies, I somehow slept right through their cries. In fact, she thinks I'm making it up half the time I hear Bailey grunting. But if you listen very carefully, you can hear the slightest of rumbles coming from her.

It's funny how different dogs communicate in their own ways.

Tessa was a talker. When she wanted something from me, she didn't bark or whine. Instead, she would make eerie sounds that seemed human. She would "talk" to me when she was ready to be fed, or when she wanted to play, or when she wanted something else from me. Like Bailey, she would sit and stare right at me, then start her talking.

Have you seen those videos on the internet of the dog that says "I love you" in dog speak? Tessa talked in the same style, but she never figured out how to form words. I am sure she was trying though because she worked so hard at it. I thought it was funny when she did that, so I would start laughing, which in turn ticked her off and made her even more animated. She would get up and wag her tail and talk and talk and talk. But she never barked when she was trying to tell me whatever it is she wanted me to do.

Yes, Tessa did bark. She would bark at the neighbor dogs, the UPS driver, and at any strange vehicle that came down the driveway. And boy did she bark when we were getting ready to go hunting. None of which I had any problems with. Luckily, she wasn't like some dogs I have known that just bark to hear themselves bark.

But when she wanted me to do something, she really did talk.

As I think back to some of the other dogs I've had, they communicated in their own way too. My yellow Lab Sierra wasn't much of a barker. When it was time to be fed, she would wrangle the dog dish and stand at the back window, staring inside. She was just hoping someone, anyone, would notice that it was dinnertime. You could set your watch by Sierra retrieving the dog dish at five o'clock because that was when we would feed the dogs. Meika, our German longhaired pointer, would rarely bark unless it was dinnertime, and then she would sound off at the back door until someone would come and feed her.

The barks and the dish retrieval at dinnertime were pretty obvious forms of communication. I knew what the dogs wanted and gave them their dinner. Tessa's talking was a little more complicated. I listened to her for years, and while many times I determined what she wanted, that was not always the case.

And then there is Bailey and her quiet little grunts. It is a whole new dog language that I am continually trying to decipher. The early morning grunts I think I have down. The daytime grunts will always be a work in progress. I'll keep trying because I am sure Bailey will keep grunting. Just like a little pig.

Occasionally, people will ask me for dog-training tips. They know I hunt birds with dogs, so they ask for advice on how to train a dog to hunt.

First, I am probably the last person they should be asking for dog-training advice. I have never really trained a dog in my life. And frankly, I have very little knowledge on how to do so. If someone is serious about training their dog, for hunting or otherwise, I suggest they go online, research the hundreds of books and videos out there, and then start doing some reading and watching.

My philosophy on having a good, healthy relationship with any dog is to first buy a puppy from a reputable breeder who offers the genetics you are looking for. That way, you will be a long way down the road toward having a good pup. If you are looking for a hunting dog, get one with the pedigree and health clearances that will put your mind at ease.

Hunting dog or not, take the time to teach the basic commands. If you can get your dog to sit, stay, come, heel, and load up, you are well on your way.

Finally, if you want a dog that hunts, you need to get it into hunting situations. Put them in those situations early and often. If they have the genetics to hunt, just getting them out hunting will light the fire that is in them already.

If you are looking for a well-mannered family dog, let them be around the kids and family as much as you can. They'll soon fit in as part of the "pack."

I have written about this occasionally over the years. And I have gotten some letters and emails from others who believe I am doing my hunting dogs a disservice by not training them the way *they* think they should be trained. That might include taking hand signals, whistle signals, and other more advanced training.

Now, I have nothing against those who want to spend that extra time prepping their dogs for field trials. But frankly, I would put the ragtag bunch of hunting dogs my friends and I have up against any of the whistle-trained dogs I have seen. I bet our mangy group would shine bright. For the most part our dogs hunt close, and they all find and retrieve birds probably better than the professionally trained dogs. In fact, I would just as soon not hunt with the hunters who need to blow referee whistles at their dogs all the time. The wild pheasants we hunt use those as their notification to skedaddle post-haste.

I have been called a "rock chucker" more than once, and I suppose I wear the name proudly. It doesn't bother me a bit to have to occasionally direct my retriever to a bird they didn't see go down by throwing a rock to where the bird is.

That hasn't happened once with Bailey since she was about two years old. Early on, as most dogs do, she learned to stop and watch a bird when it flushed, then try to mark it if it fell. She's not the best "marker," meaning she sometimes starts searching short of the fallen bird, but almost always she will quickly widen her search if she doesn't find the bird.

During our daily game of fetch, she learned, out of repetition, to take some directional hand signals when searching for her ball. I'll tell her "back" if she needs to move farther out, and will point my arm left or right depending on where she needs to go. It didn't take her long to learn those signals, even when they came from an untrained dolt like me.

When I first tried using hand signals in the field, I was flabbergasted when it worked. I guess I shouldn't have been. Again, Bailey is very smart. I just thought it might take her longer to apply our backyard skills to the real thing.

The first time we used hand signals, my friend Merle Shuyler and I were hunting along a deep creek when we got into some quail. I dropped a couple birds on our side of the creek, and Bailey and Merle's Lab Molly found them. The two dogs retrieved them, no problem.

Then I shot one that was zipping across the creek, but neither dog saw it. It was a classic rock-chucking situation.

Before I started looking for something to throw though, I told Bailey to fetch, and pointed across the creek. She obliged by traversing the nearly vertical bank, clambering across the creek, climbing up the other side, and then turning to look at me. I said "back" and pointed to the left, toward where the bird had fallen. Off she went. Within ten seconds, she had the quail and was on her way back with it.

It was cool to see. I think Merle was even impressed.

There is a reason most bird hunters rely on dogs. Even average hunting dogs make us more successful. And smart dogs, like Bailey, make us look like geniuses. When she got back to me with the quail, I wanted to kiss her.

In the years since that first find with the assist of hand signals, Bailey has been directed by this old hunter's hands more times than I can count.

Bailey is built for speed and endurance. I, on the other hand, am not. At least, not anymore. When we hunt, Bailey's athleticism poses a challenge for the older, slower member of the team. Thirty years ago, I could have kept up with her most of the time, but now that I'm in my sixties and slightly overweight, I struggle at times to keep her in gun range.

Luckily, Bailey will point. And she will hold a point as long as the bird doesn't move. This allows me to get up to her and prepare for a shot. Unfortunately, especially with pheasants, the vast majority of them just don't hold that long.

When they do though, it's incredibly exciting. Bailey goes on point, and the anticipation builds to a crescendo in a heartbeat. Most of the time, the bird that ultimately takes flight is a hen, which is not legal to shoot. Once in a while, however, a colorful rooster will burst from the brush. If you ask me, there is no prettier sight in the outdoors. The beauty of the scene is topped off by Bailey retrieving the downed bird to me before taking off in search of another.

Luckily there are still places where there are enough birds to hunt. North and South Dakota come to mind. And we've also had good luck hunting in Central and Eastern Montana. Especially for a young dog, nothing helps build their confidence and draws the hunting instinct out of them like finding lots of birds.

As Bailey grew and matured and learned, she became a better hunter. That is the case with most every dog, I suspect.

Bailey's determination is second to none. When she gets on the scent of a bird, she doesn't give up until it flies.

One of her first seasons, I watched her twice get on a running bird and track it for over a half mile before finally flushing it. Those are the kind of pheasants we deal with here in Washington State. Even during my younger, more fit days, I couldn't have kept up with her. I know some dog owners who can call their dogs off a bird in a situation like that, but even now, there is no stopping Bailey.

Over the years, Bailey has retrieved dozens and dozens of birds. Several retrieves have been really memorable.

The first, most memorable retrieve came during her second year of hunting pheasants in Montana. My oldest son Kyle was along on this hunt, his first year of hunting with his less dominant eye. During the previous year, Kyle had a couple eye surgeries to repair a detached retina. Because the eyesight in his left eye was not good enough, he had to switch from shooting left-handed, which was his natural way of shooting, to right-handed. Frankly, I don't think I could make that kind of switch, but he did and did it pretty seamlessly, all things considered.

Anyway, we were hunting along a cattail-filled ditch when Bailey froze on point. I told Kyle to be ready, and as I spoke, a rooster busted out thirty yards ahead. When Kyle shot, you could see the bird dip, telling us he'd hit it, but it just kept flying down another ditch. Then, eighty yards out, it sailed below the ditch line and out of sight.

Bailey, for some reason, sped after the bird. Normally, I would have tried to call her off, but I thought if she did happen to see where the bird went down, she might find it.

We waited only a couple minutes before we saw a little black dog pop up on our side of the ditch, running with the wounded pheasant in her mouth. That bird filled Kyle's limit for the day, and we were all proud of him. I was also proud of Bailey for finding that rooster.

A slower dog would have never kept up with the bird long enough to see where it went down.

After that day, Bailey has saved me (and a few of my hunting buddies) several other rooster pheasants when we've only winged them. She's run for hundreds of yards through corn fields and giant weed fields. By sheer determination she has found them. Every time it happens, I tell whoever will listen that this is why we feed our dogs all year long.

That is not the truth, by the way. If Bailey and I never hunted another day, we would be okay. We'd miss it, for sure, but Terri and I would love her just the same, and she'd still be sleeping on couches and eating cooked meat every meal.

Hopefully, there are many more hunts in both of us. I'm not sure who loves it more, but I can tell you my trips wouldn't be nearly as enjoyable or fulfilling without Bailey by my side.

Most people give their dogs human traits, which may be wrong or right. No need to debate that here, but I guarantee you every dog has its own personality. Bailey is different from all my other dogs, and she has some funny little quirks that none of my other dogs ever showed.

Being a Labrador retriever, Bailey is first and foremost a water dog. Or, she is supposed to be a water dog. Unlike all my other Labs before her, however, Bailey doesn't really like the water. Oh, she'll jump into a lake or ditch if she has to, but if she's not retrieving something, or going through water to retrieve something, she pretty much avoids all water.

My other Labs, most memorably Tessa, would search out water. That was especially true if they were hot, and sometimes just because. Whether it was a stinky mud puddle or the Pacific Ocean, Tessa and my other Labs would get right in.

Tessa's favorite thing to do in the summer was to search out a running sprinkler. On the other hand, watch Bailey move through the backyard, or through the orchard when the sprinklers are running, and you will see her running in a serpentine fashion like she is trying to avoid land mines. She hates it when she gets even a few drops of water on her back. It's as if she'd been waterboarded as a young pup, although nothing could be further from the truth.

I exposed her to water at an early age but never forced her in it. To this day, if you throw her fetching dummy in a lake, she'll make a champion dock dog look like a rookie with her high-flying, leaping plunge. But if you are just walking along the bank of a pond or a lake while out hunting, she'll tippy-toe around the edge, not even touching the water when she gets a drink.

If Bailey does get wet, well, she'll expend plenty of effort drying off as quickly as possible. If we don't rush her into the laundry room when she comes in after getting damp, Bailey will start rubbing on the furniture and squirming on the carpet to dry herself off.

Believe me, that does *not* go over well with the lady of the house. To avoid this, I will rush Bailey into the laundry room and give her a thorough drying with one of the "dog towels." Unlike a typical Lab, Bailey is not needy when it comes to affection, but bring the dog towels out, and a wet Bailey will embrace your touch until the last drop has been wicked away.

Incidentally, and I am sure it is merely by coincidence, I have discovered the ragged dog-drying towels in my stack of shower towels after Bailey wandered through the house wiping her wetness on the couch, loveseat, and possibly even some of our bed clothes. Payback? Me thinks so.

One year, when we were hunting in Montana with some friends, I discovered that Butch Schlagel's little black Lab, a littermate of Bailey's, also is not fond of being wet. As soon as we were back inside the motel room after a morning's hunt, Butch's Lab Bella ran over to him and enjoyed every second of a complete drying off with her special towel. Must be in the genetics.

You would think a black dog in the baking summer sun would want to get wet and cooled down. I assume most do. Not my black dog. In fact, on one summer day when the temperature in our area hit an all-time record of 115 degrees, I decided I would step outside for a couple minutes just to feel the heat. Of course, whenever I go outside Bailey must accompany me, and she immediately lay down in the grass, twenty yards from the sprinkler, in the direct sunlight!

I looked at her and thought, surely, she won't stay there long, but she was there for at least three minutes. When I finally called her over to where I was standing in the shade, I could barely touch her back: that's how hot it was. She didn't seem to be bothered in the least.

When we do come back in the house after a short afternoon walk, Bailey will lie on a vent in the kitchen that blows cool, air-conditioned air. It didn't take her long to figure out how to cool off in a non-watery way.

By now, I've had enough canine experience to know that no two are alike. But when you have a water dog, with genetics that have been carefully selected through decades and decades of breeding, those genes don't always trump their personal preferences. Bailey would still rather avoid the water at all cost.

Even if it is a record heatwave.

One of her other little idiosyncrasies is that Bailey eats lying down. All my other dogs would stand up to eat, but not Bailey. Of course, she's a different kind of dog when it comes to eating. Most of my other Labs would eat like they hadn't seen food in a week, wolfing it down as quickly as possible. Not Bailey. Half the time, she'll walk up to her filled dog dish, give it a sniff, and wander off to lie down.

When the spirit to eat finally moves her, she'll go to her dish, daintily pick up a piece of chicken, bring it into the living room, and eat it. Once that passes the taste test, or primes the eating pump, she will saunter back to her dish and lie down for a casual dinner. She'll pick up each piece of chicken and each kernel of kibble, then chew it thoroughly before swallowing and picking up another piece to eat. It might take her fifteen minutes to eat her dinner as she lounges on her belly, dog dish between her front legs. My other dogs were sometimes done eating in less than a minute.

After she eats, Bailey will stand up, belch a couple of times, wander back into the living room, lie down, and relax for a few. Then she'll come over to me, sit down, and stare at me. It's time for her after-dinner walk, just in case I have forgotten.

Chapter 17

"Old age means realizing you will never own all the dogs you wanted to."

–Joe Gores

Over the years, I have seen dogs do some amazing things, from retrieving ducks and geese in icy water to literally running through brush that was almost impossible for a human to traverse.

There are a couple fields we hunt in Central Washington that we call "man-eaters." They are so thick and tall that there are times when going forward is not an option. But our dogs, somehow, continue to move ahead, searching for whatever might be hiding in the mass of noxious weeds. The weeds are so thick in the man-eaters that instead of being able to run through them, Bailey and the other dogs have to jump over and through them to make any headway. Not just once, but over and over and over again.

If I had to do that, I would have been in cardiac arrest after about three minutes. As it is, I normally have to high-step it, raising my feet about eighteen inches before moving each one forward. By the end of the field, my calves and thighs are screaming at me. *Stop!* they say. *Now!*

But Bailey bounces along, ears flopping, tongue and tail wagging, still looking for birds.

I've read somewhere that a hunting dog will run three to five times farther than what their human hunting partner will walk. Sometimes I think Bailey runs even more than that. I guess I should put one of those step counters on her to see how far she actually runs. It makes me tired just watching her.

I did finally buy one of those electronic dog collars for her. Not so much to correct her when she is disobedient, but to keep track of her. After the issues she had with hypoglycemic seizures, I worried that if she did have an episode and I didn't see her, I might not be able to find her to come to her aid.

The collar also helps me keep track of her as she hunts through some of the big, tall fields we hunt. Push the button on the remote in my pocket, and the collar will send out a loud "doodle doo" noise, letting me know exactly where Bailey is. If she's gotten too far but isn't tracking a wounded bird or on a hot scent, I will whistle for her a couple times. If she ignores me, I'll push the button, and the sound will almost always turn her back to me.

The collar does have electrical stimulation, a shock in other words, but I've only used it twice. The noise pretty reliably gets her attention, and she comes in search of me.

I do know that Bailey runs many miles every day we hunt. She is built for it, and she seems happiest when she is covering some ground. When she does hit a hot scent, you better lace up your track shoes, because she is off to the races.

Hunting dogs are just so fun to watch. Frankly, it's the reason I still hunt. When I see Bailey doing what she was born and bred to do, enjoying it so much, it puts a smile on my face.

If you can get by all the huffing and puffing from running so hard and long, you would see that Bailey is smiling too.

All my dogs over the years have been good ones. Some were stronger retrievers, while others seemed to have better noses, meaning they could smell the birds better. Because I got them out hunting when they were young, all of them were good hunting partners. They learned the basic commands of sit, stay, heel, and come easily, and when we were out in the field, they always kept an eye on me and didn't venture too far.

Bailey has been an exception to this rule. Early on she was so determined to find the bird, she forgot about her human hunting partner. As she has aged and matured, she has gotten better. Still, she is the most focused and hard-hunting dog I have ever had, and at times that has been a challenge.

As I write this, Bailey is seven years old. Even though she is starting to get a few gray hairs on her chin, she is in her prime. Luckily, she has slowed down since being the puppy that would blaze through a field before the rest of us had a chance.

I am really looking forward to the next few years to see just how much better she does. Already, I would put her up there as my most determined and hardest hunter. Is she the best dog I've ever had? I don't know.

It's hard to rank the dogs in my life; it's like picking a favorite child. You love them equally. Each one has their strengths and weaknesses. So, as I think about all the dogs I have been privileged to live with, and to hunt with, I won't rank them. They were all good in their own ways.

Bailey will most likely be our last dog. It makes me sad to think about that. I have loved hunting with dogs throughout my life, and the idea of not having another Lab at some point in my future makes me start thinking about a time I no longer will have the ability or desire to hunt.

It's not just the hunting either. A dog adds so much to life in general. They quickly become every bit a part of the family. During the best, and some of the hardest, times in my life, a dog or two has been there too.

I remember Zeb playing with Kyle and Kevin throughout their early years. Kyle was two years old when we picked up Zeb as a puppy. As puppies are apt to do, Zeb grew quickly, and the boys weren't far behind.

Cassie and Meika came into the family and grew with the boys through their middle school and high school years. The dogs loved having the boys throw the ball for them and later hunted with the boys as they started their journeys as young hunters.

I will never forget taking a nine-week-old Tessa over to my parents' house after we brought her home from Nevada. My dad was in the later stages of Alzheimer's, but I can remember him smiling and reaching out to pet our little yellow puppy as I held her out to him. She licked his face, and he smiled some more. He was pretty much beyond communicating at that point, but still, the smile said it all.

The boys are grown now, out making lives of their own. As I write this, our youngest son Kevin and his wife Joi are expecting their first child, a baby daughter. It will be our first grandchild. It is an exciting time, for sure.

At home now, it is just Terri and me . . . and Bailey. That little black Lab has done what none of our other dogs could do. Bailey has won Terri's heart. We do more worrying about Bailey and where she is and what she is doing than we did with all our other dogs combined. And that, in a nutshell, is the issue.

As Terri and I settle into our retirement years, being able to do some traveling without having to worry about Bailey would be nice. Yes, she could travel with us, since she is a good traveler. Still, finding motels that are pet friendly, or heaven forbid, trying to travel by air with her, makes it just seem easier to stay at home.

Not that we will be rid of Bailey anytime soon. I hope to be hunting behind her for many years to come. I want her lying at my feet—or in Bailey's case, on the couch next to the fireplace—for as long as possible. Having a dog in the house makes it more alive, warmer. A dog makes it a home.

Based on the life span of my other dogs, Bailey has another five or six years left on this earth, and a couple more than that if she is lucky. I hope to have a few more than that too, but who knows what the grand plan is. Dogs just don't live long enough. We all know that their lives are too short, even when the little ball of fur with the sweet-smelling breath lands in our laps for the first time. Blink, and the puppy is all grown. Blink again, and they have gray on their muzzle.

It gets increasingly difficult for me to decide when a dog is ready to leave this world for the next one. Bailey will be the most difficult yet, if and when it is up to me to determine if it is time for her to leave us.

No, there will not be another dog in my life. Bailey is it. And she is maybe the perfect dog to end with. She's smart, sweet, incredibly easy to live with (if you stick to her daily schedule), and of course, she is a great little hunter.

If my granddaughter and any other future grandchildren read this, I hope they will discover that their old granddad had an awesome life, filled with the love of a great family, lots of wonderful friends, and with the incredible companionship of several special dogs. Each one was a loyal friend and hunting partner. Wouldn't it be great to know we might meet again someday?

I never knew I wanted a dog when I was a kid. It's not that I didn't want a dog, I just didn't know any better. Boy am I glad the dogs showed me differently. A life without dogs is a life with some giant holes in it if you ask me. My time on this big rock has been enriched by the unwavering love of all the dogs mentioned in the pages of this book.

And I've enjoyed time with dozens of other dogs over the years too. Dogs of my friends and hunting companions. All were a joy to watch and be around. They have all been entertaining, for sure.

Some of the best memories in my life include those I've shared in this book. But there are many, many more. Days spent hunting around the West with one dog or another. Nights sharing motel beds with exhausted dogs in small towns here and there. There are other memories too, like taking an afternoon breather in the shade of a tree or walking three miles back to the truck in a blizzard. One or more of my dogs were part of each of those too.

Sure, the great shots on fast-flying birds and amazing retrieves by this dog or that all pop up in my memory bank. But so do the incredible sunrises viewed over a pond of decoys or the walks along a ridge as the sun sets after a great afternoon hiking through the Cascades in search of blue grouse. My dogs were there so many days in the field, it is hard to list them all.

I believe I have a lot of life yet to live. With many more memories to make. Up to this point, however, I'd have to say it has been a life well lived. Made so much better because it has been shared with some really great dogs.

Afterword

I have written over fifteen hundred newspaper columns for the *Yakima Herald-Republic* since 1991. Most of the columns have revolved around outdoor pursuits: hunting, fishing, camping, shooting and more. Occasionally, I have written about something my dogs have done or something that has happened to or with them. Of all I have written, the dog columns get the most response from readers, almost all favorable. People, whether they hunt or not, like to read stories about dogs—or so they tell me. They either have a dog or had a dog in their life, and the stories bring back fond memories.

You've read some of these stories, re-written in the previous pages of this book. But there are many others that were favorites of mine and my readers that I thought might be appropriate to include here. Bonus material, you might say. I hope you enjoy them.

–RWP

On Dog Intelligence

There was an article in the paper the other day about how German scientists have determined that some dogs have the intelligence of a three-year-old child.

Now, I'm not sure how long the study was or how much money was spent on determining what a dog's IQ is, but I could have saved them a whole lot of time and money. In fact, I've said it many times before, my three hunting dogs act like three-year-old kids quite frequently.

My oldest dog, a twelve-year-old German longhaired pointer named Meika, can be the biggest child of them all. And she can be a cranky old lady too. I don't know where that fits on the intelligence quotient scale, but there are times that you would swear she was ninety, and other times she acts like she is three.

The other two dogs in the Phillips' household are the ever-popular Labrador retrievers. One is black, and one is yellow. The black lab, named Cassie, may have some questionable lineage. She looks to me as if somewhere along the line a collie or a shepherd may have jumped the fence and became involved in the gene pool. Her little ears, big body, and different shaped head all make her look just not quite all Lab. But she is all black, and she loves to hunt and retrieve and would do anything to please me. In fact, she is almost like the perfect little three-year-old child, always standing by my side and watching the other two dogs play, or more often than not, get into trouble.

The yellow lab, named Sierra, actually is three years old and may be the smartest of the bunch. At least, she is the most conniving of the group. Probably because she is the youngest in body, she is the one that is always instigating a game of tag or hide-

and-seek with the older dogs. Even if the two older dogs aren't interested, Sierra will pester them until one or both join in a game of romping around the yard.

Three-year-old kids will nap, and my dogs can nap with the best of them. In fact, when the day is done, unless we have been out hunting, my dogs will out-nap any three-year-old kid.

Sharing and playing nice can be a real problem for three-year-olds. Sharing and playing nice can be difficult for my dogs as well. Because she is the youngest and the fastest, my little yellow lab can almost always get to the tennis ball before the other dogs. And even though I have three tennis balls, one for each dog, they all three seem to want the same ball. If Sierra has the one favored ball, then Meika will whine and cry and howl until she gets it. Sound like a three-year-old?

The funniest part of the whole deal is that when Sierra has the ball that Meika wants, she will actually take it over to her and prance in front of her and show it to her like, "Neener, neener, neener, I have the ba-all!"

Which makes Meika whine and moan all the louder.

And, similar to a three-year-old child, my dogs cannot sit still. Which can be a real pain in the duck blind. Maybe it is because we don't hunt ducks all that often, but sitting still in the duck blind is absolute torture for them. Instead of sitting patiently and waiting for the next duck to come in, they will stand, sit, stand, walk in a tiny circle, sit, stand, etc.—all the while whining softly.

But my dogs love to go. When they are loaded into their boxes in the back of my truck, they know that something fun is about to happen. I'm sure if they were sitting in the back seat of a car and could actually speak, they would be constantly asking, "Are we there yet?" or "When are we gonna get there?"

If there is too much standing around between drives through the asparagus field while pheasant hunting, they start to get impatient and are ready to go hunt some more. If they had little hands that they could use to tug at a trouser leg, they definitely would be doing that while asking, "Can we go now?"

My dogs are normally not too naughty, but once in a while they will get into trouble. I think boredom is what creates most of the mischief. If they are tired of playing or napping or chasing the birds in the arborvitae bushes, they will occasionally dig a hole big enough to bury a Smart car. Or they will chew on the fence boards. Normal three-year-old kids won't do that, but they certainly will find something that gets them into trouble when they are bored.

Now, I'm not saying that my three are the smartest pooches in the world. But you can look into their eyes and see some intelligence. They tell you when it's time to eat. They know when you are going hunting. And they always seem to be in a good mood, even if I have just hollered at them for digging—or chewing or whining or barking.

I see hunting dogs on TV that can do multiple retrieves using only hand signals and whistle blasts to direct them to where they need to go. And there are dogs that will sit patiently by their master's side without moving a muscle or making a sound for hours on end.

Mine won't do any of those things. Not because they aren't smart enough, but because I haven't worked with them on doing so. I'm sure if I took the time, they could learn to do many things.

In the meantime, however, they are quite content at teasing each other, taking naps, and whining when they don't get their way. No scientific study needed here; my dogs act just like three-year-olds.

On Doggy Dreams

I'm sure that sometime in the past, someone, somewhere has done studies on the sleeping habits of dogs. It was probably even financed by the government using our tax dollars. I guess I really should look it up on the internet to be more informed, but I have heard that dogs, on average, will sleep around twenty hours a day. If the researchers were to take my three dogs as a case study, they might find that to be off just a tad.

My two older dogs, a thirteen-year-old German longhaired pointer and a ten-year-old black Lab, probably sleep more like twenty-two to twenty-three hours a day.

On the other extreme, my four-year-old yellow Lab may sleep as little as two hours a day. It is hard to tell really, because every time I look out at her, she is wide awake, ears alert, tongue hanging out, looking in at me as if to say, "Let's go somewhere and do something." Even in the middle of the night, if I stumble out of bed to get a drink of water, there she will be, sitting on the patio, watching me wandering into the kitchen.

No matter what time of day or night, if I take one step towards the back door, she is up and prancing, usually with a tennis ball in her mouth, just waiting for me to come out and throw the ball for her, or take her for a walk, or, in a perfect world, take her hunting. In a better-than-perfect world I would come out and feed her, and then take her hunting, and then come home and feed her again.

All of this ruckus from Sierra will awaken the black Lab, who is just gullible enough to buy into the whole, "Oh boy, here he comes, we're gonna get fed or get to go hunting" routine, and she will, in turn, start barking and prancing.

Meika, my old pointer, is either too old to care or smart enough to know better because often she will just lie there and sleep right through Sierra's excitedness. Of course, it doesn't hurt that she is nearly deaf. Or at least I think she is. I know there are times when I holler at her that she just flat doesn't hear me. On the other hand, she might just be smart enough to be faking deafness or old enough to not care.

I do know Meika can sleep. And she will sleep long and hard. There have been several times recently that I will look out in the yard, and she is out cold. And she will stay that way for incredibly long periods of time. Long enough to make me think that she has finally just died. I've had to walk out and make sure she was still breathing more than once in the past few months. And happily, I guess, I'll find that she is still alive, and within seconds she is up and hunting the yard for her favorite tennis ball.

It is often said that we give human traits to our pets, but I know that dogs must be like people in some ways, including the amount of sleep they get—or don't get. Some dogs need more, and others can live with a lot less. I have dogs on both ends of the spectrum.

Again, I haven't researched this, but after watching my dogs go into sound-asleep fits that involve growling, whining, and some tremendous paw-flopping and leg-jerking, I assume dogs dream while they sleep.

Of course, dogs have no way of telling us if they do dream or what they are dreaming about, but I have to believe, watching my dogs practically run in place while they're asleep, that they have some good ones. Do they dream about past hunting escapades? Or are their little brains creative enough to be making up things, like humans do in our dreams? For instance, do dogs dream of showing up at obedience school wearing, gasp, only their underwear? Or do they dream that they are chasing some car, and no matter how hard they run, they just can't quite catch it?

While they are asleep and fidgeting and yipping, are they dreaming that some monster cat is chasing them and just about to pounce on them? Or are they hot on the trail of a running rooster pheasant? Wouldn't it be fun to know?

I like to think that my dogs are dreaming about some of our past hunts. Is Meika dreaming about the time a couple years ago that a rooster pheasant actually held for her as she pointed motionless at the end of a snow-covered asparagus field? Does she, in her dreams, see me walking up past her and kicking the weeds until the big, colorful bird flushes into the December sky? And then does she see herself picking the bird up and retrieving it to my hand? That's the way it happened, and hopefully it's replayed that way in her dreams.

And was Sierra dreaming about running through the tall grass in Mott, North Dakota last fall as she jerked and whined during a rare sleep a while back? Did she relive the three days of running and smelling and flushing and retrieving pheasant after pheasant? I hope so.

Is Cassie, my black Lab, dreaming of retrieving ducks on the Columbia River? Or is she excitedly flushing quail along the Yakima River as she shakes and quivers and barks muffled barks in a moment of fitful slumber?

I suppose I should do a little research to know for sure even if dogs can dream. I'm sure my taxes have helped fund a study on the subject somewhere along the line. My guess is that no matter how much they have studied the sleep habits of dogs, they still don't know for sure if or what they are dreaming.

It makes me feel better thinking my dogs are dreaming happy dreams. Not to add to the problem of giving human traits to our pets, it's just that is what I would want to be dreaming if I were a dog.

On Tennis Balls

After some thirty-odd years of dog ownership, I have learned a few things about our four-legged friends.

Now, I am by no means a dog authority. Nor do I profess to be any kind of an expert dog trainer. But after dealing with a motley assortment of hunting dogs over the past few decades, I have gained a little knowledge about dog behavior, as well as human behavior as it relates to man's best friend.

If you are considering buying a dog in the near future, or have just obtained a new puppy, may I be so bold as to pass on a helpful hint that might assist in the nurturing of a pet, companion, hunting partner, or whatever you want your dog to be.

The first and foremost thing you should know is that dogs (especially retrievers) should never be introduced to tennis balls. And I mean never.

Tennis balls are to dogs what HGH is to Barry Bonds. Once they have experienced it, they gotta have it, all the time.

I have made this mistake several times. And with each new dog I have told myself that I would never do it again. But somehow, I have succumbed to their desire for a tennis ball to play with.

The big question is, are dogs pre-programmed to want a tennis ball even though they have never seen one before? My theory is this is the case.

It must be similar to a walleye wanting to eat a night crawler. Think about it, when would a walleye ever see a night crawler? But put one on your hook and send it to the bottom of the Columbia River, and the walleyes will gobble it up.

Stick a bright green tennis ball in front of a Lab's nose, and the dog will go—pardon the pun—ballistic.

Over the years I have had dogs, including my old German longhair pointer and three different Labs, that would want you to throw a tennis ball for them until they literally couldn't run anymore out of sheer exhaustion.

My current Lab will grab the ball and actually throw it at me. If I don't catch it, she'll go retrieve it herself and bring it and throw it at me again. Over and over, she will play the game until I finally throw it for her or she tires herself out.

My German longhaired pointer will bring the tennis ball to me, drop it at my feet, and then back up four or five steps and stare at me with these longing eyes. If I don't throw the ball within thirty seconds, she starts barking at me. And she will continue to bark until I acknowledge that the ball is at my feet by either picking it up or kicking it.

When I am mowing the lawn, she has learned that if she drops the ball in the path of the mower, I have to stop and kick the ball out of the way. A half hour of lawn mowing will take an hour because of the "kick the tennis ball out of the way" game.

My first Lab, a yellow dog named Zeb, had the annoying habit of keeping the tennis ball in his mouth all the time, finally jamming the thing between your legs when he wanted you to throw it for him. Taller people would get the wet nose and slobbery tennis ball about mid-thigh. Shorter people weren't as lucky.

And you didn't want to be sitting in a lawn chair when Zeb wanted to play ball because he would deposit the slimy, dirty ball right in the middle of your lap, Grandma's white capris be damned.

Putting a tennis ball in front of a retriever is like putting a twinkie in front of a fat kid. They can't resist it.

Oh sure, all the hunting dog experts tell you that retrievers should never be worked or trained with a tennis ball. Their theory is that the dogs tend to bite down hard on the ball, and it gives them a "hard mouth." They feel like if a dog learns that it can bite down hard on what it is retrieving, it will automatically bite into the gamebirds they are fetching.

All of my tennis ball retrievers have also been great bird retrievers, and all have had very soft mouths. So, I don't buy into the hard-mouth theory. And I've known hard-mouthed dogs that have never seen a tennis ball in their life. That's not to say that they don't know about tennis balls, because I think they do.

Somehow, they know, and they want a tennis ball. When they see one, they will do anything to get it. It's like putting a rack of ribs in front of Pavarotti.

I have a variety of other retrieving dummies that I use when working with my dogs. But put a pile of bumpers and fake duck and pheasant dummies out in the yard along with a tennis ball and invariably a dog will grab the ball if given the choice.

The best remedy to the situation is to never, ever get your dog started playing with tennis balls. Even if they give you the most pleading look with those huge, hard-to-resist brown eyes, stand firm. It is an extremely tough task, but you must resist or you will create yet another tennis ball retrieving monster that will never relent.

This is just a small bit of advice from someone who knows. May the force be with you.

On What Dogs Have Taught Me

When my German longhaired pointer, Meika, and I were invited to be on a new Outdoor Channel television show called *What the Dogs Taught Me*, I should have realized that that would be one of the questions the host would ask me during our day in the field. But I hadn't really even thought about it when Scott Linden popped the question about what Meika had taught me during our years of hunting together.

As usual, when I am asked a question for which I am unprepared, I stuttered and stammered and probably even "uhhhed" and "ummmed" a few times. I can't remember exactly what it was I said, but it had something to do with paying attention to Meika, as she almost always knows more about what the birds are doing than I do.

I've had time to think more about the question since we did our videoing last fall, and the more I ponder the question, the more I realize that dogs can teach us plenty. And not just in the field or duck blind. Yes, I am partial to hunting dogs, but I have known a number of other dogs too, and all of them could teach us plenty if we would just pay attention to them.

Probably the first thing that we can all learn from dogs is that no matter how crummy a day it has been, there is always something to be happy about. With my three dogs, this happiness usually focuses around feeding time. They may have had the worst day ever. It may have rained all day, keeping them confined to their houses, but even on the darkest, dreariest day, they are all tongues and wagging tails come supper time. In the wake of all the things going on in our world, even after a crappy day at work, we should be happy to have a home and something to eat. That is how a dog would look at it.

Another thing we can learn from our dogs is that, even during the toughest times, we should attack each new task with excitement and renewed vigor. Anyone who has hunted with dogs knows this to be true. You may have spent all morning hunting through fields that held no birds whatsoever. Or you may have sat for hours in a duck blind without hearing a single quack. But head to the next field, or get up to pull the dekes, and the dogs are as hopeful, positive and ready to go as if none of the poor hunting had even occurred. I can't say as much for most people.

Because of their scenting ability, dogs truly do know more than we do in the field, and we need to pay attention to them all the time. Every hunter I know has, at one time or another, ignored or not trusted his hunting dog when the dog was acting birdy and paid the price of missing a bird. Some of us who are slow learners have had this happen to us several times.

I can think of several occasions when friends and I were walking back to the truck after hunting through a field and the dog, or dogs, have disappeared. Most of the time we have not paid attention to where they went or what they were doing, and sure enough, they will have found and flushed a bird.

I remember one time hunting with my old Lab Zeb, when he went on point out in the middle of a bare field. In the first place, Zeb was not a pointer. My only thought was that he had seen a mouse or something. Plus, I could plainly see that there was no bird in the short grass and dirt. There was simply no place for anything bigger than a cricket to hide. So, I just kept on walking. That was the wrong thing to do. A second or two later, a nice rooster pheasant erupted from out of nowhere, and I was too flabbergasted to even shoot.

Finally, what may be the most important thing I have learned from my hunting dogs over the years is never leave them cold, tired, and hungry in the back of the truck alone with a limit of quail. Raw quail tastes just as good to a dog as a nicely cooked one does to us. Oh, and after a severe scolding if something like that ever does happen to you, know that dogs are much quicker to forgive and be happy with you than you are with them.

Hopefully, I will be invited to be on the TV show again sometime. If I am, I'll be ready with a whole bunch of good answers to the question about what dogs have taught me. That is if I can remember them. If not, there'll be plenty of very intelligent "uhhhhs" and "ummms," I'm sure.

On Dog Names

A friend asked me the other day about any thoughts I might have regarding the naming of a hunting dog. He and his wife were about to go pick up a new chocolate Lab pup, and they were trying to figure out what they should call the new addition to their family.

I told him that naming a dog is not to be taken lightly. Choosing the appropriate moniker for your pooch may be even more important than naming a child. Because, while you probably aren't going to be frequently out in public screaming your kids' names at the top of your lungs (okay, some of you might be), there is a very good chance that you will be doing just that with your hunting dog, possibly over and over again.

So, selecting the right name is very important.

I had always heard that the best names for working dogs are single-syllable names that are easy for the dogs to learn. Names like Buck or King or Duke are such names. All good strong names that even the hardest-headed or most intellectually challenged dogs should be able to understand.

That always made sense to me. So, I named my first dog Zeb. And that seemed to work just fine. It was short, easy to say and rolled off the tongue quite nicely when being screamed in a sentence such as "ZEB, GET BACK HERE, YOU LONG-RANGING, NO GOOD, SO AND SO!" (Or words similar.)

Actually, Zeb was a pretty good dog, but like every dog, he had his moments, and if I had had the wherewithal to purchase one of those electronic training collars, Zeb would have been my best dog candidate for such a device. Then I could have just yelled, "ZEB, HERE!" and if he didn't cooperate to the fullest extent (which was often the case), I could have reached out and touched him with a little reminder.

My next dog was named Sam, and even though Sam was a she, and Sam is more thought of as a male's name, Sam was the perfect single-syllable name for her. I never had to raise my voice to Sam. She just hunted hard and minded well so she could have been named Queen Elizabeth the 27th, or we could have called her "it" and she would have been a great hunter.

After that I strayed off the single-syllable name path and named my next dog Meika. Then my next Lab's name was Cassie, and my latest dog actually has a three-syllable name. Her name is Sierra.

All of them have no problem knowing their names, although all have had their bouts with selective hearing loss and have had to be called more than once.

I now hear that some dog experts are saying that a multi-syllable name is actually better because that way the dog's name can't be confused with any of the single-syllable commands that you want your dog to learn. Not that anyone would name their dog "here" or "sit" or "stay" or "heel," but I guess some names could be confused with those commands, although I can't think of any right now.

Some people who are really into hunting name their dogs appropriately. Buck is an appropriate name for a hunting dog. Some family friends had a black Lab named Buck, which was short for Buckshot. Other good hunting reference names for hunting dogs that I have heard include Drake, Gunner, Scout, and Tracer.

I have also heard of hunting dogs named Mallard and Rooster. To me, those are just too clever and, in my group of hunting buddies, would become very confusing. The guy who owned Rooster would scream his name, and everyone else in our group would mount their shotguns and say, "Where?"

I once hunted with a guy who had really given his hunting dog's name some thought. He named his hard-hunting little springer spaniel Artemis. According to this guy, Artemis was an ancient god of hunting, and he thought that was a great name for a hunting dog.

I think it would be cool to have a dog named Artemis, but the first time someone saw me running out through the corn fields screaming, "Artemis, Artemis," they would really think I'd lost it, and "it" is not a hunting dog.

Affixing the appropriate moniker to your canine is an important task. Does the number of syllables matter? I don't think so. How it sounds being screamed from a duck blind or in a wheat field on a fall afternoon may be a better criterion.

By the way, sometimes the names of the guys you are hunting with can get confusing as well. One time a group of buddies and I, with a whole pack of dogs, were hunting pheasants in the breaks of the Snake River. We were pushing one of the draws up to a couple of posters, one of whom was named Ken.

Now, as most pheasant hunters know, when a pheasant gets up, someone will yell "hen" or "rooster" if the birds are flying toward someone else in the field, just so they are aware of what sex the bird is. Wild hen pheasants are illegal to shoot in Washington State (and everywhere else as far as I know), so it's considered a courtesy to let the rest of the hunters know that the bird flying at them is a hen just in case the sun is in their eyes or the lighting is poor.

We were just about to the top of the draw when one of the dogs flushed a hen. The guys doing the pushing started yelling, "Hen! Hen!" We watched as the bird flew right by Ken and then, bang, down it went.

When we got to the posters, we saw Ken holding the hen. He had a very embarrassed look on his face.

"What happened?" one of the guys asked.

"When I heard you hollering my name, I knew it had to be a rooster," Ken said.

On Driving with Dogs

I was sitting at a stoplight the other day when a car turning left into the lane next to me started swerving my way. I was getting a little anxious as the car kept veering my way and was starting to think about some way to avoid the pending collision. I tried to make eye contact with the driver of the other vehicle, but to my surprise all I could see was a dog standing in the driver's lap, totally blocking his view of me sitting in the turn lane.

At the last second, the guy swerved to avoid me, a big smile on his face as he obviously thought it was humorous that the dog standing with his head out the driver's window was enjoying his own version of a game of chicken.

Now, I love dogs as much as the next person. Maybe more. But allowing a dog to sit in your lap while operating a motor vehicle is more than just a little bit stupid. Unfortunately, I see dogs hanging out the driver's window or sitting in the driver's lap almost every day.

According to a survey by the American Automobile Association, over 80% of dog owners drive with their pets in the car. There are 43.3 million households with pets, so that is an impressive number of people on the road with dogs in their vehicles.

Surprisingly—or maybe not based on almost getting dog-crunched the other day—some 17% of those who drive with dogs in their car allow the dogs to sit in their laps as they drive. Talk about distracted driving. Tell me you would be able to react quickly enough to avoid an accident with a dog wrapped around your arms or bouncing from leg to leg. Or what happens if you do have to quickly turn or brake? Little Fluffy sitting on the edge of the window will be shot out of the car in an instant.

Again, I realize we all love our pets, and we probably allow them to do things we shouldn't, such as sleeping on the couch or eating too many treats. But allowing them to ride unsafely in a vehicle is not spoiling them; it is putting their, and YOUR, health in danger.

I learned that lesson the hard way with my first hunting dog. He was a yellow Lab named Zeb, and to get him from home to where we hunted I would have him jump into the bed of my pickup truck where he would sit, or stand, and ride.

One time, however, he decided that something smelled so good that he needed to jump out of the truck as we were traveling down the road. Luckily, it was on a sharp turn when I had slowed down considerably. In my side mirror I saw Zeb bail over the side of the truck. Fortunately, I was able to stop quickly to get him loaded back up without causing an accident. None-the-worse-for-wear, besides a little road rash from landing in the gravel bar ditch, Zeb learned a valuable lesson that day. As did I. From then on, he rode in a dog box that not only kept him contained, but also helped keep him protected from inclement weather.

According to the Humane Society of the United States, some 100,000 dogs are killed each year in accidents involving riding in truck beds. In addition, veterinarians all over the country see cases of dogs being injured because they jumped out or were thrown from the bed of a pickup truck.

Other injuries can occur just from allowing the dog to stick its head around the cab of the truck or out the window of a vehicle. For some reason, dogs hate to have you blow in their face, but they love having the sixty-mile-an-hour wind buffeting their mug. I am sure the thousands of smells hitting the olfactory sensors is the reason why.

It's just not a good idea to allow it, however. Think about how many times a rock or large insect has smacked your windshield when traveling down the road. Now think about what kind of damage that could do to your pup's eye or face if one of these projectiles were to hit it. Kind of scary, isn't it? But it happens. More frequently than you might think.

There are safe ways to secure your dog for a ride in the car. Many animal groups recommend restraining your pet in car seats just as you would a child.

Hunters have many good options for a safe ride for their dogs. A dog crate of the appropriate size is perfect for allowing your pup to ride to and from the hunting grounds, whether it be a few miles down the road or three states away. With a padded mat or a soft bed of straw, my dogs have ridden safely and comfortably for hundreds and hundreds of miles in their travel crates.

A few states and some cities around the country have now made it against the law to drive with a dog in the operator's lap. It's too bad laws like that are needed. It seems common sense would override the need for yet another traffic law.

Dogs are definitely man's best friend. But doggone it, they are terrible drivers and need to stay out of the driver's seat.

On Christmas Gifts for Dogs

Here's an interesting little tidbit. Last year, Americans spent $16 billion on their pets. That's billion, with a "b."

Those billions were spent on over-the-counter medication, and supplies such as clothing, toys, leashes, beds, and other accessories.

Wait, what? Clothing?

Yep, it seems we—and by we, I mean lots of other people who aren't me—spend our hard-earned money on clothing for pets that, because they are animals, don't need clothing.

And now that the Christmas season is here, it seems that spending on our pets skyrockets.

I'll be the first to tell you that I spoil my dogs. But in all the years of dog ownership, never have I purchased an item of clothing or spent a dime on a Christmas gift for any of them. My dogs are smart, but to my knowledge, they have no concept of what Christmas is.

Yes, they understand that there is now an evergreen tree planted in the living room where there most recently was a stuffed chair. And there are some funny lights surrounding the front garden area where, in the summer, a gray digger lives. But never once have they shown the slightest interest in opening gifts with the rest of the family. Admittedly, every Christmas I can remember, the dogs napped comfortably on their doggy beds, of which I have purchased dozens and dozens over the years, adding to the giant pet supply economy.

Now, that's not to say our dogs haven't had an item or two under the tree. Because they have. As much as my wife Terri suggests my hunting dogs are sometimes more trouble than they're worth, she has a soft spot for anybody and anything not getting a gift. So, there will invariably be a chew toy or stuffed animal there for the dogs on Christmas morning.

I remember her buying a Christmas stocking for Bailey when she was just three months old. It was a cute little stocking with a big "B" on it. When Terri put the stocking down for her to check out, Bailey immediately went to town on it. Within minutes, the bright red stocking with the fluffy white top was torn to shreds.

The only time I remember the dogs showing any interest in the gifts under our tree was the year our yellow Lab Tessa was just six months old. While we were away at a get-together, she jumped the baby gate and started scrounging through the gifts under the tree. She discovered a bag of miniature Snickers bars and proceeded to tear it open and eat them all, including many still in the foil wrappers.

For several days following, we had shiny reflective droppings sprinkled around our backyard.

Even though Terri might think otherwise, I know that our dogs couldn't care less if there was anything under the tree for them come this Christmas morning.

On the other hand, let me get my hunting boots and shell vest out and head for the door without them, and they'll raise a ruckus that would awaken even the soundest sleeping spouse. That, they understand and care about immensely.

By the way, so does Terri, but that's a story for a different time.

Maybe I am just a tight wad or a little cold-hearted, but buying a Christmas gift for the pooches seems frivolous. Not that I won't spend money on them. Tessa now is the bionic dog. I have lost track of the thousands of dollars I have spent on her in surgeries and treatments and drugs to help make her life more comfortable.

Luckily, Bailey has been pretty healthy. Still, between training collars and chew toys and premium dog foods and Scooby Snacks,

I've put a few bucks into the booming economy surrounding pet product purchases.

Evidently, the really big buyers of pet stuff are millennials. Especially the high-earning ones. According to one survey, millennials will spend an average of $183 dollars on their pets this holiday season. That is more than my parents spent on me for Christmas throughout the bulk of my childhood! The big spending for Christmas is most likely tied to the trend known as "humanization," where pet owners increasingly treat their dogs, cats, and gerbils like members of the family.

Of course, pet stores are trying to cash in on the trend, with many rolling out products specifically targeted as special Christmas gifts for our four-legged family members. To that I say "bah." I won't add the humbug because I do love our dogs. My way of showing them that, however, is not by purchasing them a Christmas gift, but by getting them outdoors as often as I can. When you see the joy in Bailey's face and in her bounce when she is in the field looking for pheasants, there is not a gift in the world that could be its equal.

Not even a sweater.

On Daylight Saving Time

So, I guess I am a little early. Or wait, am I little late? I have to tell you this most recent time change has me boogered up. It's never affected me much before, but for some reason this time it is getting to me. I was waking up at 5:30 or 6:00 a.m. during daylight saving time, and now I'm waking up at 4:30. For the past few nights, I've had to talk myself out of heading to bed at 8. For crying out loud, how old am I?

My dogs have played a part in this situation. They have an internal clock that is as accurate as the upgraded world atomic clock. At precisely 5 p.m., they are ready for their dinner. If it gets to be five minutes past, they are getting a bit worked up. And at ten minutes after, if they haven't seen our dog-feeding ritual starting, well, they become quite concerned. Concerned enough that their humans need to be barked at, with one dog bouncing up and down, and the other sitting right in front of you and staring like she is trying to bore a message into your brain.

Of course, with the time change, that fun little ritual gets started at 4 p.m.

Sometimes we're not home at four, so I am not sure what they do. I guess they lie in the backyard and dream about eating.

My older Lab, Tessa, has developed a bad habit of needing to go out some time in the middle of the night. It could be as early as 11:30 or as late as 3:30, but some time in that four-hour period, she will raise a ruckus and need to be let out for a few minutes.

Sometimes her need to go out coincides with my need to get up to use the bathroom. But most of the time she is waking me out of a dead sleep. I haven't done the research, but I think sleep doctors will tell you it's not all that great for your physical being to be interrupted every single night, sometimes during REM sleep.

I was hoping that with the time change, if I could get Tessa out for one last walk, say around 10 p.m. or so, she would be able to make it through the night, at least until 5. So far that's not happened, because come 10, I have been asleep for at least an hour.

My younger Lab, Bailey, functions more like a farmer. When it gets dark, she is ready for bed. And as soon as the first signs of light show in the east, she's ready to get up and start her day. Now, with the change back to standard time, and it getting light soon after 6 a.m., Bailey is in my face, wanting to go for a walk, followed by our morning play time.

Believe me, there's no rolling over to get another fifteen minutes of sleep. Bailey is determined that this is what we do, and this is when we do it.

I don't care how hard you try to explain to them that the clock has been turned back, they are not buying it. Their clock tells them when it is time to eat and time to play, and when you aren't listening to their clock, they will pester you to no end.

What's that old saying? You can't teach an old dog new tricks. I beg to differ.

Somewhere along the line during the past year, I started giving Tessa a bite of chicken or steak or burger after we were done with our dinner. I figured meat was good for her, so as I would take the dishes to the sink, I would slip her a bite of whatever meat I had left on my plate. I did it a couple times, and it quickly became routine. Now, if—heaven forbid—I don't give her something as I clear the table, she is all over me, reminding me that she needs her bite of post-people dinner food.

It's funny to watch Tessa, as she gets quite animated over the whole deal. Bailey, on the other hand, just coyly sits and watches, letting her big sister be the harasser. Then, she'll gladly take a small bite of meat too.

If I still wore a watch, I could set it based on the dogs and their daily rituals.

This change of time has definitely affected me more this year for some reason. I partially blame it on age, but mostly I blame it on the dogs. They don't understand it, and frankly they're not standing still for it.

So, let me apologize in advance if I'm early or late for whatever. Unlike my dogs, my internal clock is all fouled up. And it looks like it might be for some time to come.

On Talking to Dogs

Okay, I'll admit it, I talk to my dogs as if they're humans. And the funny thing is, I think they know what I'm saying, at least some of the time.

Now, like a proud parent who thinks their kid is the smartest little darling in the world, I am of the belief that one of my dogs, my little black Lab, Bailey, is pretty smart. And my other pup, a yellow Lab named Tessa, picks up on some of the words I am saying, or is smart enough to know that when Bailey goes, so should she.

I know it didn't take Tessa long to understand that when we are out hunting, and Bailey hits a hot bird scent, or better yet, goes on point, she needs to get over there and get her nose into the business too.

Recently, I've been playing with words to see just what kind of reaction I can get from the dogs. It is pretty amusing, and sometimes amazing to watch.

The Phillips' dogs quickly learn the basic commands. Words such as sit, stay, and come are pretty automatic unless, in Bailey's case, she is just too busy to come when she is asked. She's like a spoiled four-year-old who always is making excuses for not doing what the parent asks them to do. With her actions, Bailey is saying, yes, she hears me, but she just needs two more seconds to check something out here, and oh, there is something interesting right over there she needs to smell.

Usually, a stern "COME" is all it takes to let her know I am serious about her coming. Usually.

In doing a little research, it looks like even dogs with average intelligence can understand maybe more than we think. According to Dr. Stanley Coren, an expert in canine intelligence, the average dog can understand about 165 words, possibly more with training. He says consistency is the key, making sure you use the same word for an item or a command every time. If you want the dog to come, use the word "come" or "here," but stick with one or the other.

In thinking about it, I am not too sure how many words Bailey and Tessie know. I am guessing just by watching the two, Bailey knows more though. For instance, I can say the word "lizard," and Bailey gets almost apoplectic and runs to our retaining walls to look for the different lizards that inhabit the rocks and blocks. Tessa just sits there.

In Tessie's defense, being eleven years old with a serious case of arthritis in her back legs, she just may be smart enough to know that chasing the quick little lizards is like chasing the wind. It's a lot of wasted energy. Let the stupid kid chase them.

And Bailey does. She has chased them for three years and has yet to catch one.

One word that does get Tessa's attention is "treat." Say that word, even wrapped into a fifty-word sentence, and she perks right up. She might be dead out in one of her lengthy naps, but say the magic word and, boom, just like that, she is wide awake and looking for a treat.

Bailey definitely knows what treat means because she will wander out, slowly, like a hundred-year-old tortoise, to the treat bucket when she hears the word. And she will eat the treat, but when it comes to food, she can take it or leave it. Literally. Our vet says that Bailey is not "food motivated." Which has to be a bit of an anomaly, especially in Labradors. But the term fits her to a T.

If you want to see Bailey motivated, just say the word "play." Or the word "fetch." Put the two together, and you will find a VERY motivated dog, although one word is usually all it takes. At one or both of those words, she is off to the laundry room where we keep the ball and thrower. She will sit there until I arrive and then she will stand on her hind legs, front feet on the counter, looking at the ball. Then she will look at me, then back to the ball, and back to me, like she is trying to say, "Right there, there's my ball, right there, see it, right there?"

Both dogs know the three-word command, "Go lie down." Which is good. And, "Time to eat" is definitely one that gets Tessie going.

"Bedtime" is another one that they know. Say those two words, and off they go to their beds.

I can think of a dozen more, but I am not sure I can come up with 165. My dogs may not be as smart as some. That's okay. They do pretty much what I want them to. They enjoy life immensely and they make me smile every single day. What more could you want?

On Chuckits

The British are wonderful people. They've invented all kinds of helpful things. The steam engine was invented in England in 1801, and the British developed the lawn mower in 1827. They invented the tin can, linoleum, and the jet engine, among many other items that have helped mankind. It seems a group of people who enjoys eating haggis, kidney pudding, or jellied eels can pretty much come up with anything.

One of the more recent inventions out of England is a little device called the Chuckit. This simple but unique tool has saved me and many other dog owners around the world all kinds of pain and suffering.

A Chuckit is an unassuming device that allows the user to throw a tennis ball with ease. And by its design, it allows even semi-coordinated people to toss the ball a good distance.

Over the years I have had many different hunting dogs, and virtually all of them have been retrievers. And what do retrievers want to do? They want to retrieve. It is what they live for. Until fairly recently, I have never used any kind of an aid to throw something for my dogs to retrieve.

Then I discovered the Chuckit.

Okay, I know the gadget, which looks like the offspring of one crazy night of mating between a backscratcher and an ice cream scoop, has been around for a while. I just never thought I needed any assistance in throwing a ball for the dog. That realization came after we moved out into the country where our dogs could run literally a hundred yards or more if someone could throw something that far. Brett Favre, maybe, but me? No way!

So, after suffering from tennis-ball-throwing elbow for a few months, I decided to try to find something to help.

The first thing I found was a mechanical launcher that uses a .22 caliber shell to shoot a special retrieving dummy out for retrieval. The launcher works great, and for those of us who are training a dog to be good around gunfire, the deal is perfect because it makes a loud bang when it sends the dummy into the air.

The only downside to using the launcher is you have to extract the shell casing and put a new one into the unit each time you want to throw the dummy. The shells, which don't include a bullet, just gun powder to propel the dummy, aren't cheap. So, if you have a dog that never seems to tire and wants to play fetch several times a day, using the launcher can get tedious and somewhat expensive.

My little Lab, Bailey, is just such a dog. She's built for speed and endurance and would play fetch until you about threw your arm off. Or broke the bank buying launcher shells. She loved the loud launcher, but it just wasn't an everyday toy.

Then one day I was wandering the aisles at Cabela's, looking to buy a couple more training dummies when I saw this odd-looking thing called a Chuckit. It cost all of about eleven dollars, so I thought, "Why not give it a try?"

In the past six months, Bailey and I have about worn the thing out and have gone through about two dozen balls.

The Chuckit comes with a bright orange tennis-style ball that is recommended for use with the thrower, but regular old tennis balls will work too. The Chuckit I have is about fifteen inches long and does a great job of lobbing balls good distances without much effort. The arm of the thrower is just flexible enough that it adds extra speed to your throwing motion and really flings the ball. Backhand, side arm, underhand, overhand, the Chuckit throws the ball with relative ease.

I see that there is now a longer version of the Chuckit, which must add even more distance to the throw. Bailey would enjoy running even farther, but I'm not sure our small orchard could contain a much longer throw.

We often play and train four times a day. If I had to throw a ball or training dummy over and over again, well, I just couldn't do it. But with the assistance of the Chuckit, I can throw for fifteen minutes or more without even feeling it.

Now, I know there are some dog trainers out there who will tell you not to use tennis balls for training purposes. We don't. We use training dummies for the training times, but when we just want to play and get some good exercise, the Chuckit is my go-to gadget.

I'm not sure about bangers and mash, or mushy peas on toast, but the British do come up with some good creations now and again. Whoever it was that came up with the ball-throwing tool called the Chuckit, I would like to give a hearty "cheerio!"

On Christmas Gifts for Dogs, Part Two

Someone asked me the other day what I've bought my dogs for Christmas. I had to think about it for a second. Actually, I didn't have to think about my answer, I had to think about the question.

In nearly forty years of dog ownership, I have never purchased anything for my dogs for Christmas. I know, all you dog-gift-buyers out there probably think I'm a Grinch. But if you asked any of my dogs, past or present if they've felt slighted in any way, my guess is they would just cock their head and stare at you like they have no idea what you just asked. Besides having a strange tree in the corner of the front room and lots of bright red decorations placed around here and there, they wouldn't know Christmas from Arbor Day.

So, to answer the question, I haven't purchased a thing for my dogs for Christmas.

Not that I don't buy stuff for my dogs. Because I do. On my last trip to Costco, my bill was just over $100. All but $11 of that was for treats and vitamins for my dogs. And, unfortunately, that is not unusual. Between bully sticks and beef chews and chicken treats, along with some canned sardines, my basket almost always has more for our four-legged family members than the humanoids.

Not to mention dog food. I started the unbelievably complex search for just the right dog food for Bailey, my sleek little black Lab, who runs constantly and only eats sparingly. Trying to figure out what combination of duck, chicken, beef, lamb, and vegetables is right is a conundrum I have yet to unravel. And do we feed food with grains or not?

Then there is Tessa, my arthritic older Lab who will eat anything you put in front of her and could easily weigh 100 pounds or more if I didn't control it.

So, for a while, there I was buying two different dog foods—one at $85 for a 30-pound bag—which just about had me dipping into my retirement fund. Even today, with two different types of food for two different types of dogs, I am paying more per pound for their food than I am for the meat Terri and I eat. Our two sons are now quite fond of telling friends that their mother and I treat the dogs way better than we ever treated them.

It's not true, by the way. But we certainly treat our current duo of canines better than some of the pups that have come before them. Not that any of them were abused or mistreated. We just weren't so soft. Past dogs might only get one or two treats a day and have to be outside most of the time.

Our Labs now seem to always be munching on one kind of a treat or another, and are quite comfortable in front of the fireplace anytime we are home. And when we aren't, if it is going to be cold or snowy, they get to stay in their beds in the laundry room instead of having to be out in their nice, insulated houses on the back patio.

Most people train their dogs to do things. I have done some of that. But I think the dogs have actually trained us too.

Of course, we want them to let us know when they need to go out to pee and poo. Which they do. Bailey will come and sit down in front of me and just stare at me until I ask what she wants. She will then go to one of the doors, telling me she wants out. Or she will go sit and stare at her ball, telling me she wants to play. If she is hungry, she will go lie down by her dog dish and grunt until I come and put some food in it. And they say dogs can't talk.

Tessie, my older Lab, will also come get my attention at dinnertime. If it gets to be two minutes past five, she figures we have totally forgotten that she needs to eat and will start jumping up and down and making a fuss until we go get her dish. It's quite a routine.

It will be that way tonight, and it will be that way on Christmas. Every day is the same to the dogs, unless we get a chance to sneak away and go hunting.

Bailey is three now and has mostly gotten past the chewing and playing with toys stage, although every now and again she will find her little ducky and start flipping it in the air and shaking it. Tessa . . . she couldn't care less.

Would Bailey like a new toy for Christmas? Maybe. But my guess is it would be fifty-fifty if she would even play with it.

So, no, I won't be buying the dogs something for Christmas. Heck, around our house, every day is Christmas for them. And when we go bird hunting, it's Christmas, New Years, and the Fourth of July all wrapped in one! Luckily, during the fall, we celebrate quite frequently. What more could a bird dog want?

On Shedding

They say that Labrador retrievers only shed twice a year—spring and summer and fall and winter. In other words, it is pretty much a year-round phenomenon.

I have two Labs. One is yellow and the other is black. Tessa, the yellow Lab, will inevitably rub up against your leg or put her head in your lap when you're wearing dark pants. In an instant, you'll be covered in yellow doggy hairs. If you wear khakis or light-colored pants, somehow Bailey, the black Lab, will end up in your lap, and then you're covered in about 3,000 black Lab hairs.

No matter how much you brush the dogs, they still shed. Tessa has a downy undercoat, which comes out in chunks at times. You can fill a brush with Tessa hair almost every day of the year. When she is really shedding, you can create a ball of downy undercoat in a few minutes that I'm sure could be spun into yarn and knitted into a hat.

Bailey has a sleek black coat of hair. To look at her, you'd think she couldn't be losing much hair because if she did she would be bald. Nope, she is shedding constantly, which is confirmed by the daily dumping of the collection tray in the robot vacuum cleaner.

Tessa's hair is thicker and denser, so it stays relatively close to the ground. Bailey's hair is fine and seems to float all about. Black Bailey hair ends up in the weirdest places, including in the corners of the bathroom where she rarely goes. Once in a while, a single black Bailey hair will end up on a dinner plate. That goes over like a belch in church when one of the fine black hairs lands in the plate of Mrs. Phillips.

"Argghhh, Bailey," she will say.

I don't even ask. I know what the issue is. Bailey will just look up like "What did I do? I'm clear over here minding my own business."

I know there are dogs that don't shed. My mom had one. It was a Havanese. Molly was her name, and she didn't shed and didn't bark. I would tease my mom that if she wanted a dog that didn't do any of those dog things, she should have just bought a stuffed animal. But Molly was a really nice dog and was a great companion to my mom in the last years of her life.

A Google search will show that there are actually quite a few dogs that don't shed. Unfortunately for me, only one or two of those breeds look like they might actually hunt. The Irish water spaniel is classified as a sporting breed, loves the water, and doesn't shed.

Poodles are also on the no-shed list. I know poodles were once, a long time ago, bred to hunt. You probably would have to look long and hard to find one that hunts today.

There's another dog on the list, a Lagotto Romagnolo that is hypoallergenic, doesn't shed, and is supposedly adept at hunting truffles. Frankly, I've never heard of the breed before, but that doesn't mean much. I'm not very worldly. But looking at the dogs on the internet, the Lagottos seem to be good-looking, athletic, medium-sized dogs.

If they can find a truffle underground, they should be able to root a rooster out of a briar patch. Which brings up another concern for this and some of the other non-shedding breeds that might actually enjoy chasing a pheasant or quail around. They all have medium to long, curly coats. They don't shed, but I'd bet a day's wages that they'd be one big cocklebur after a day in the field around here.

I had a German longhaired pointer back in the 90s. She was a hunting machine, but at the end of every day in the field, I would spend at least an hour with her cutting and pulling burrs out of her coat. She hated our post-hunt de-burring ritual, but she loved to hunt so much she'd go through the agony of me pulling the burrs without putting up a fuss.

So, even though they are shedders, there are some advantages to having shorter-haired dogs. The cockleburs and other clingy weeds just roll off them in the field. And they never really require haircuts and special grooming other than a bath now and again and a good frequent brushing.

My Labs are pretty much maintenance free. This time of year, they love a dip in the lake, which helps some with the shedding. Just know, though, that if you come to the Phillips' house for a visit, you are most likely to end up with some dog hair on your clothing.

And, whether you are wearing light or dark pants, Tessa and Bailey, well, they'll have you covered.

Acknowledgments

I'd like to thank all of my hunting buddies through the years for going along with me and my dogs on some incredible adventures.

Special thanks goes to my brother Doug Phillips, who spent countless hours going through boxes of family photos to help locate some of the photos included in this book.

Image Captions and Attributions

Chapter 1: The first Phillips family dog was a nice, but obese Brittany spaniel named Scamper. She loved to hunt but her obesity made it difficult to do so.

Chapter 2: A yellow Lab named Zeb joined the young Phillips family when Kyle was just two. Zeb and the author would share many hunts and experiences over the next decade.

Chapter 3: Zeb was a great hunting partner and retriever. However, on this occasion he decided for some unknown reason that he didn't need to retrieve the final duck of the day.

Chapter 4: The black Lab named Sam came into the author's life as an adult. She was a fantastic hunter with a drive that sometimes got her into trouble.

Chapter 5: Meika, a German longhaired pointer, landed unexpectedly in the author's arms and soon was pointing a wing on a fishing line.

Chapter 6: Meika loved to hunt pheasants and would point them when they held. And she loved her human hunting partner, often times protecting him and "her" birds from other dogs and people.

Chapter 7: Cassie, the author's next dog, was a fifty-dollar Lab of questionable heritage. But she was the ultimate lover dog and a good hunter in her own way.

Chapter 8: There is nothing cuter than a puppy. This almost white yellow Lab stole the author's heart and they bonded immediately. Sierra was a good hunter and an even better member of the family for some thirteen years.

Chapter 9: Sierra was an excellent communicator, and reminded everyone daily when it was time to eat by rounding up the dog dishes and bringing them to whoever was around.

Chapter 10: Another yellow Lab joined the Phillips family next, and Tessa was soon chewing, digging and creating all kinds of puppy mischief.

Chapter 11: After developing bad arthritis in her back legs, Tessa was the subject of many treatments, including cold laser procedures that required everyone to wear special goggles.

Chapter 12: The McKimmy family thought they were buying a German shorthaired pointer when they picked out their puppy they named Jack. But Jack grew up to look more like a springer spaniel and had the odd habit of barking whenever it got on the hot scent of a pheasant.

Chapter 13: The author's son Kyle, with his great hunting Lab Cali, enjoyed many years together including some incredible hunts in Eastern Montana.

Chapter 14: Bailey has not only become a loyal hunting partner, she often spends time with the author as he writes.

Chapter 15: Among her many talents, Bailey enjoys climbing the cherry trees in the family orchard looking for fruit-stealing birds.

Chapter 16: Bailey may be the smartest of all the dogs in the author's life. She communicates everything she wants to do, or needs, through little grunts and by staring into the author's face.

Chapter 17: The author and Bailey have shared some great times hunting birds here and there. She has also become a very spoiled member of the family. Photo by Dianne LaBissoniere.

Author photo: Also taken by Dianne LaBissoniere.

About the Author

Rob Phillips is an award-winning outdoor writer and author of the bestselling Luke McCain mystery series featuring a fish & wildlife officer and his yellow Lab, Jack. Rob and his wife, Terri, live in Yakima, Washington with their very spoiled Labrador retriever.